Simply Play Piano

by

Joanne Fairclough

ISBN:978-1-8380929-3-1

Copyright 2020
All rights reserved. No part of this publication may be reproduced, stored in a retrieval system or transmitted in any form or by any means, electronic, mechanical, photocopy, recording or otherwise, without prior written consent of the copyright owner. Nor can it be circulated in any form of binding or cover other than that in which it is published and without similar condition including this condition being imposed on a subsequent purchaser.
The right of Joanne Fairclough to be identified as the author of this work has been asserted in accordance with the Copyright Designs and Patents Act 1988.
A copy of this book is deposited with the British Library

Published By: -

i2i
PUBLISHING

i2i Publishing. Manchester
www.i2ipublishing.co.uk

PREFACE

This is where your musical and artistic journey begins! Music and colour have common emotional qualities. Therefore, whilst learning to play the piano, the use of colour will brighten and stimulate your mind! Being involved in music is about having fun, being creative and achieving your desire to learn the instrument of your choice!

Internationally, the ranking of colour preference is blue, followed by red, green, violet, orange, and yellow. This book includes the blue and the red to guide you through the notation and is suitable for an absolute beginner or as a sight-reading tool. Enjoy the process of learning music whilst following this auxiliary tutor book. The skills you will build on include reading the music, building on your technique, and gaining basic theory knowledge.

All of the technical exercises and melodies in this tutor book are composed by Joanne Fairclough. Technical studies, such as scales, chords and arpeggios are combined within the pieces, therefore learning them in an enjoyable and creative style.

CONTENTS

4. Simply C-C
5. Left Hand C Major Scale
6. Simply BCD
7. Simply Treble Clef Theory
8. Simply 5 Notes
9. Simply 6 Notes
10. Simply 7 Notes
11. Simply 8 Notes
12. Simply 9 Notes
13. Right Hand Steps Up
14. More Theory Time
15. Left Hand Steps Down
16. Branching Out in 4/4
17. Simply Bass Clef Notes Theory
18. Simply Hands Together Now
19. The Echo
20. Simply 3 Beats
21. Simply a Variation
22. Time to Move On
23. Time to Sharpen Up
24. The Echo Transposed
25. Right Hand Scales
26. The Snake Charmer

27. Minor to Major
28. Broken Chord Study
29. The Music Box
30. More Scales
31. More Bass Clef Theory
32. Chord Study in C
33. A Variation on Chords
34. A Theme and Variation on 'Happy Birthday to You'
35. Let's Rock the Boat
36. Leap Frog
37. Simply Basic Blues
38. Developing Rhythms in a Scale Study
39. The Robin
40. Time to Study Arpeggios
41. Octave Leaps + The Swinging Hammock
42. Simply Add Clefs
43. Sci-Fi
44. Let's Harp On
45. Strolling Along
46. Blues Bass
48. The Lock Down Blues
50. Developing Scales

Simply C to C
The C Major Scale

* In an octave scale there are **8 notes!** (abbreviated as **8ve**)

* In the C major scale these notes are all white keys!

Notes .....C D E F G A B C
Fingers 1 2 3 1 2 3 4 5

The Treble Clef (Right hand notes) are Highlighted in Blue!

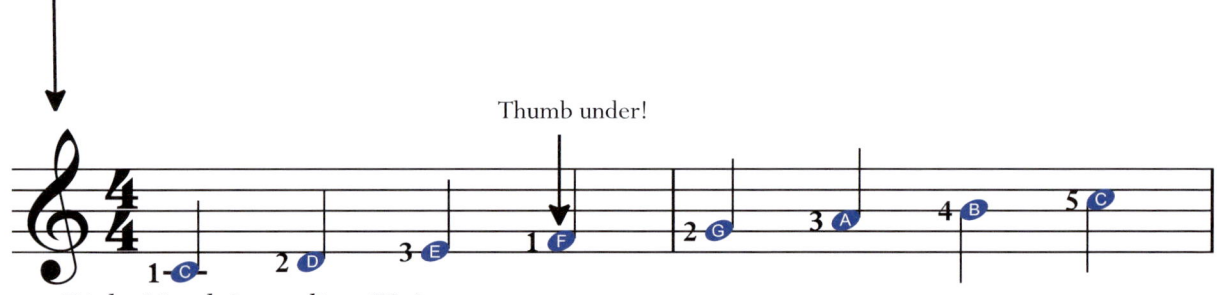

Right Hand Ascending (Up)
Start with thumb (1st finger) on middle C

Thumb under!

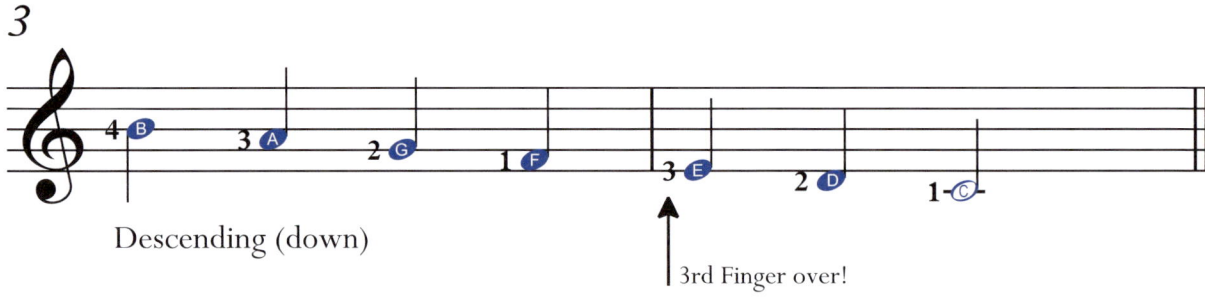

Descending (down)

3rd Finger over!

♩ = Crotchet = 1 beat

𝅗𝅥 = Minim = 2 beats

C Major Scale
Left Hand only
Descending & Ascending!

The Bass Clef (Left hand notes) are Highlighted in Red!

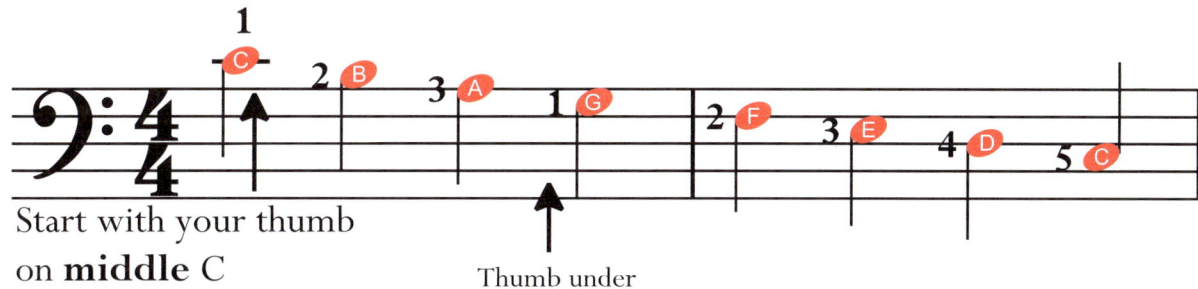

Start with your thumb on **middle** C

Thumb under

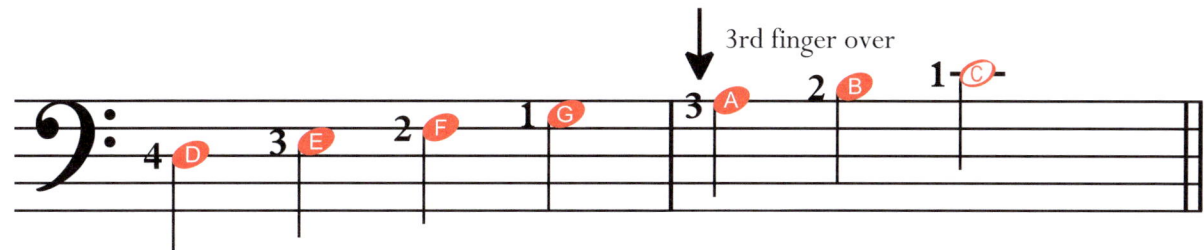

3rd finger over

Ascending
Start with your 5th finger on lower C

3rd finger over

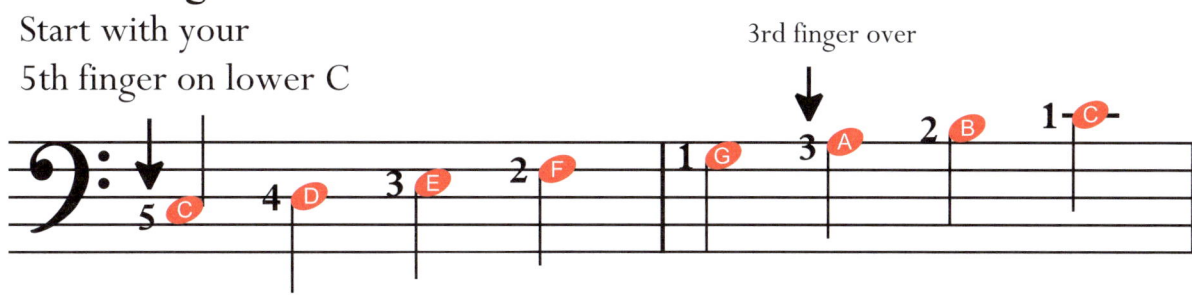

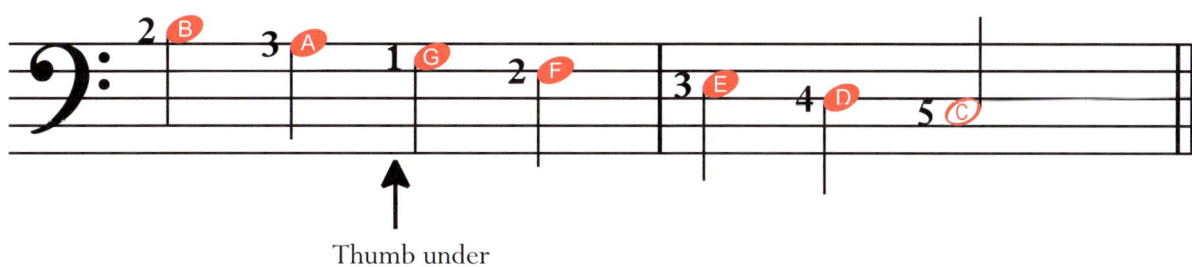

Thumb under

Simply
B C D

♩ = crotchet = one beat

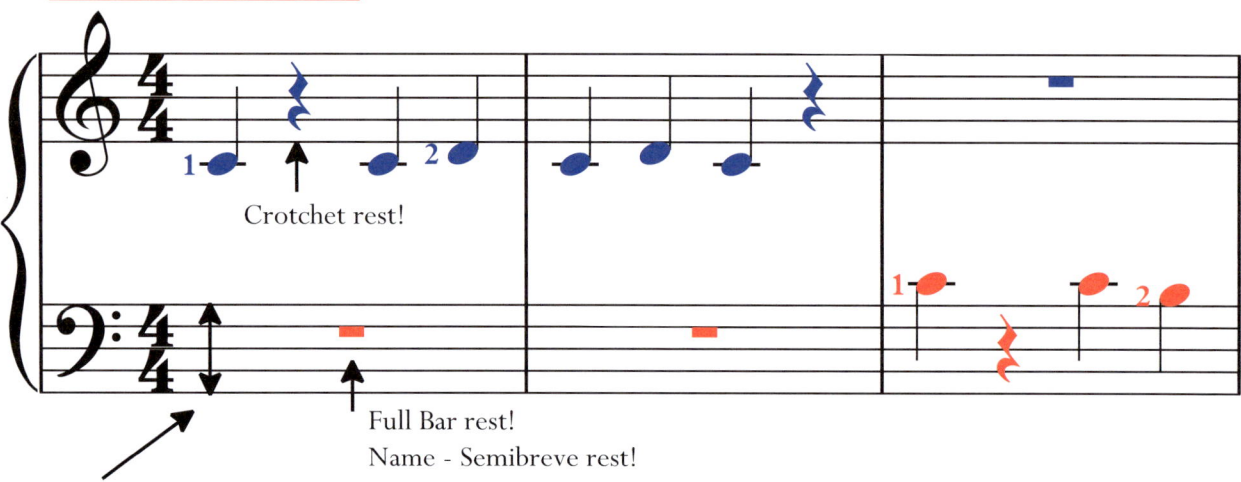

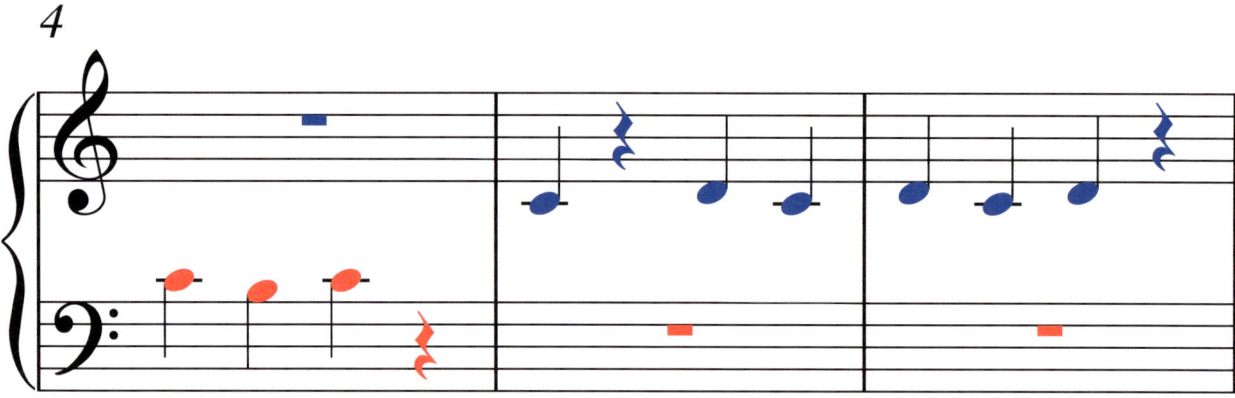

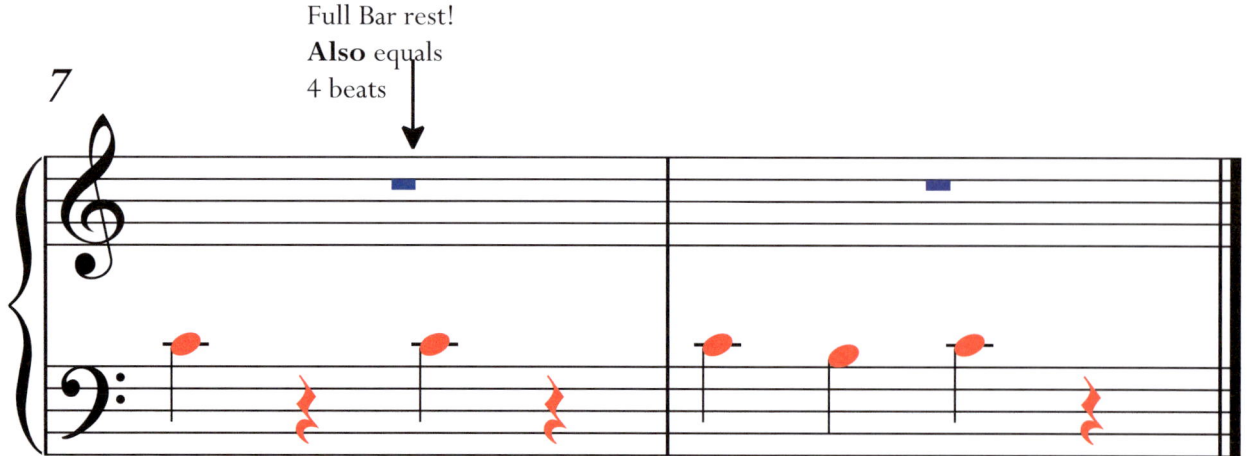

Simply 5 Notes!

Simply 6 Notes!

Left hand Position!
Thumb on Middle C
2nd Finger on B
3rd Finger on A

Right hand Position!
Thumb on Middle C
2nd Finger on D
3rd Finger on E
4th Finger on F (New note)

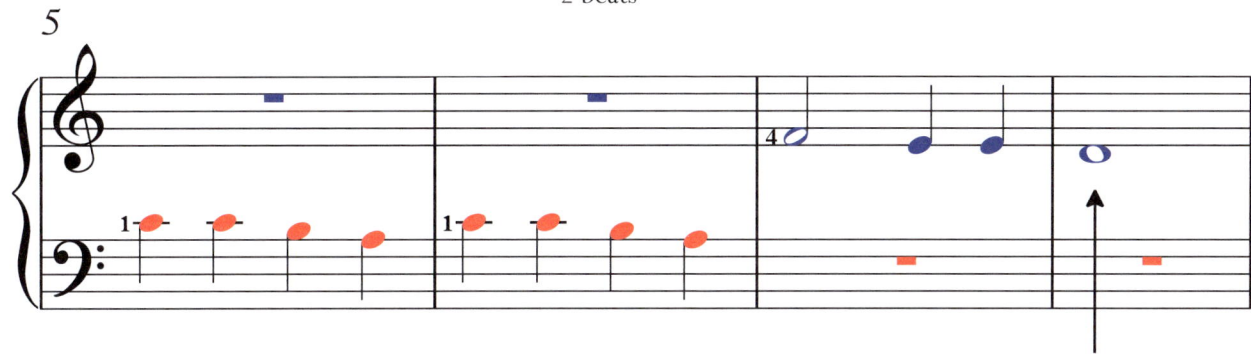

Minim note
2 beats

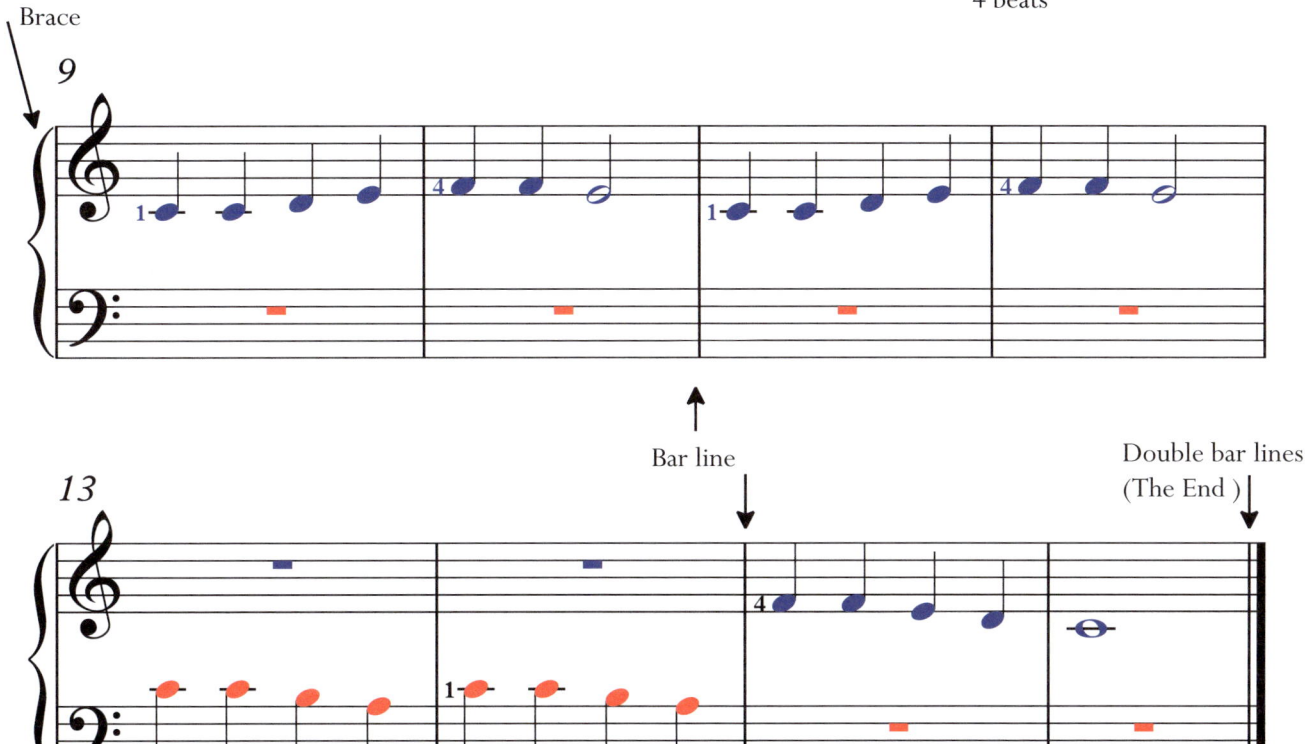

Semibreve note
4 beats

Brace

Bar line

Double bar lines
(The End)

Simply
7 Notes!

Left hand Position!
Thumb on Middle C
2nd on B
3rd on A
4th on G (New note)

Right hand Position!
Thumb on Middle C
2nd on D
3rd on E
4th on F

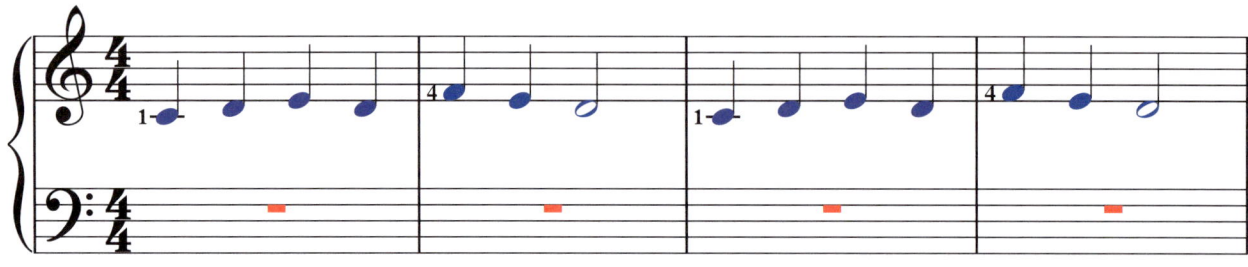

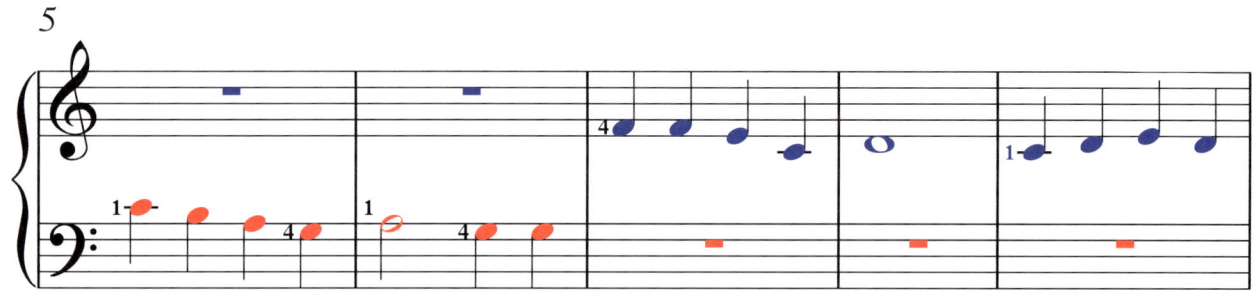

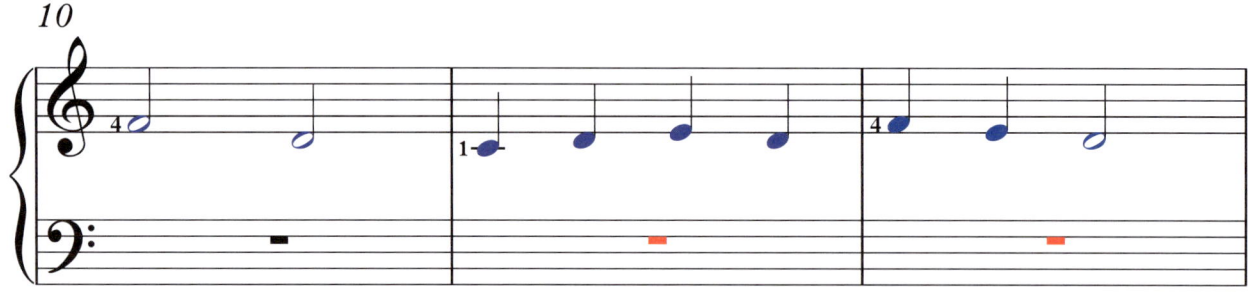

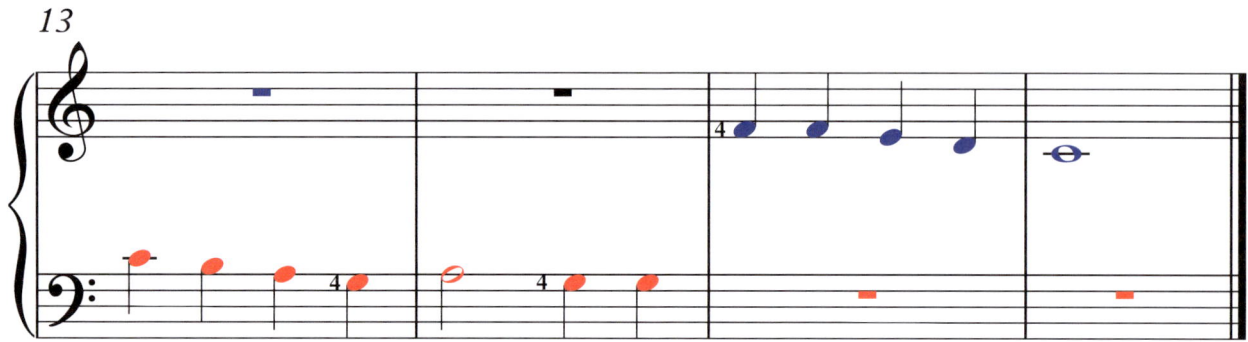

Simply 8 Notes!

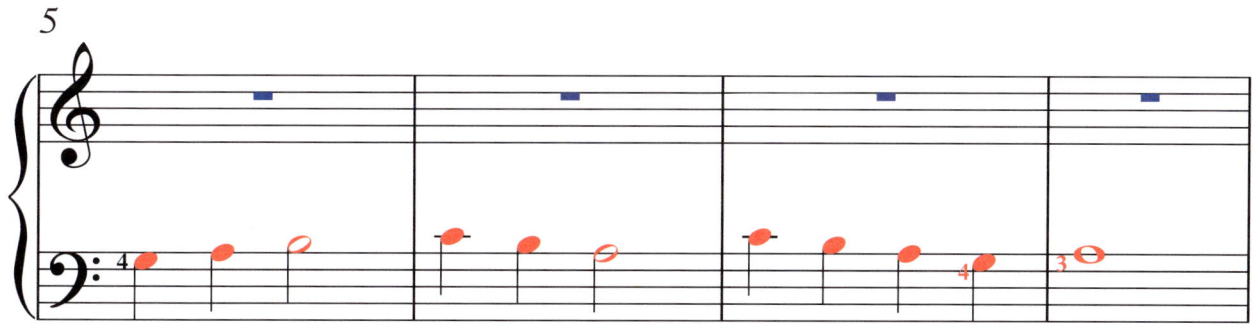
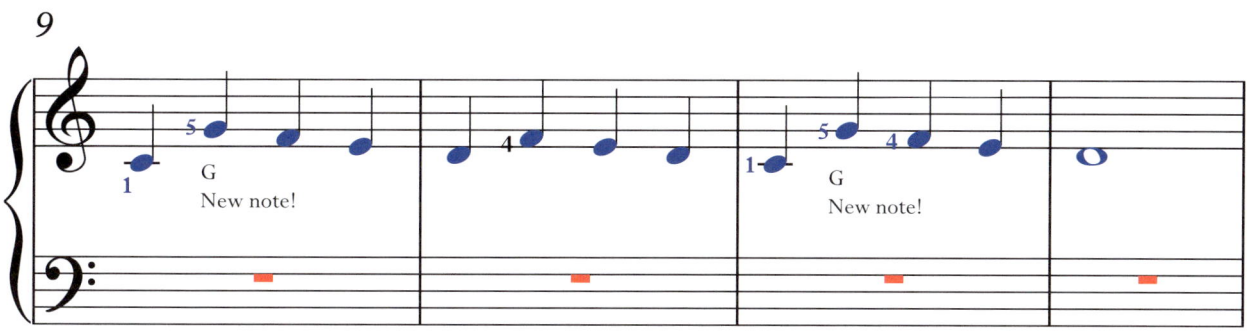
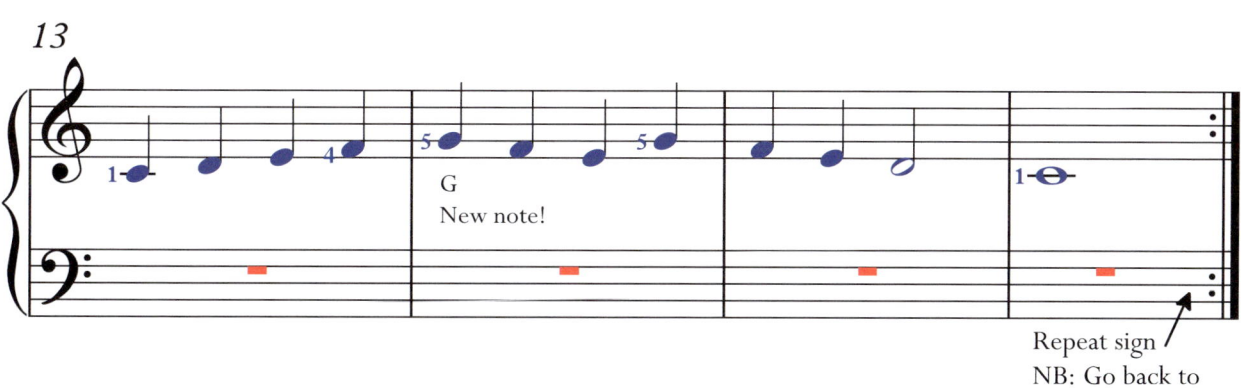

Simply 9 Notes!

Left hand Position!
Thumb on Middle C
2nd on B
3rd on A
4th on G
5th on F (New note)

Right hand Position!
Thumb on Middle C
2nd on D
3rd on E
4th on F
5th on G

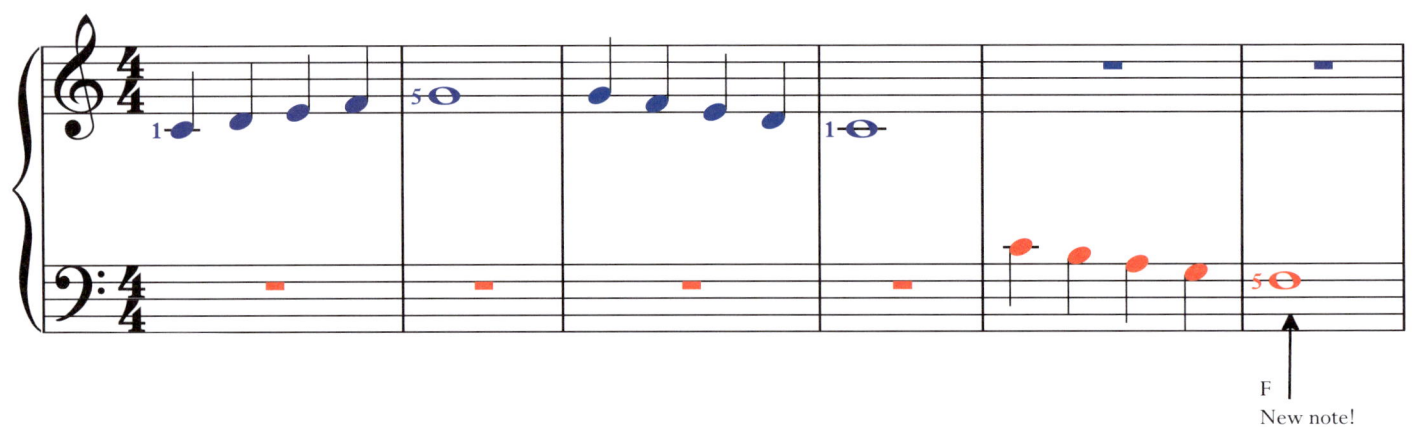

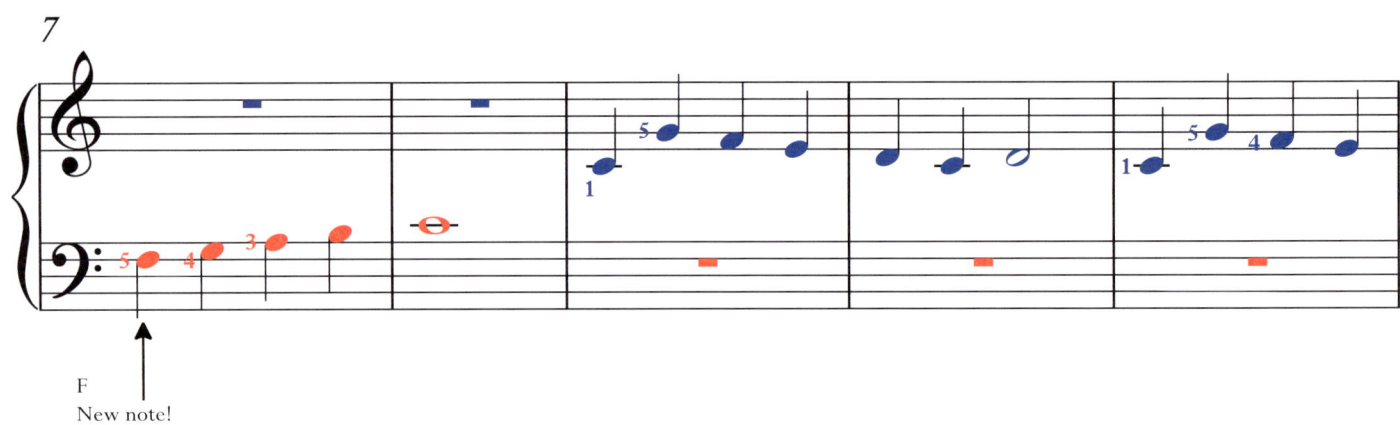

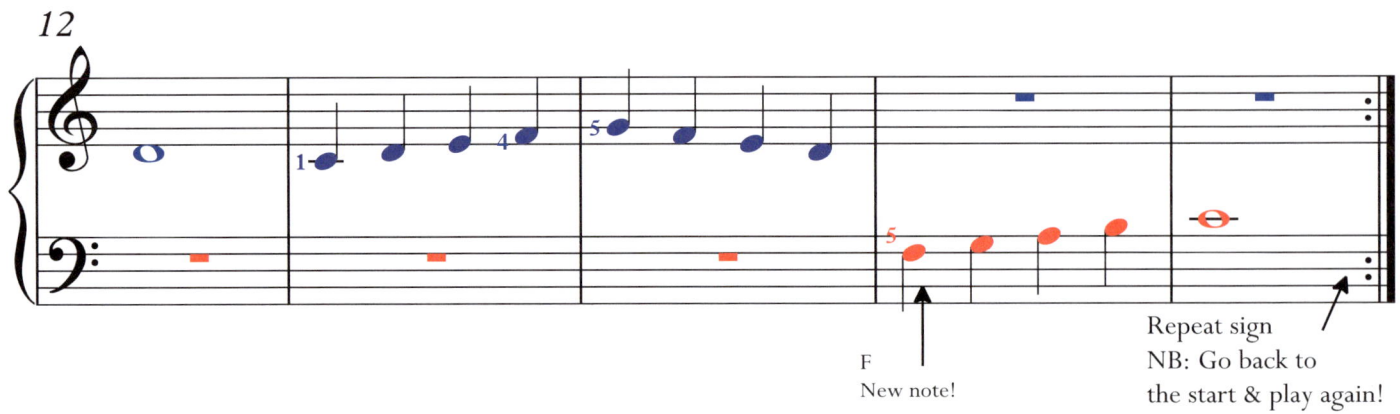

Right Hand Steps Up!

1★ Read the note names **before** you play them!
2★ Say them **as** you play them!

1st Finger(thumb) begins on C
then moves to D, then E and F

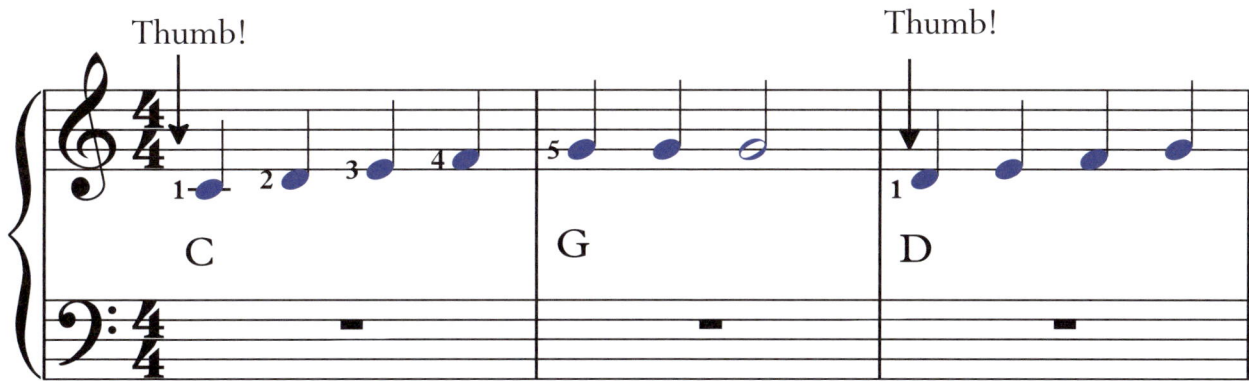

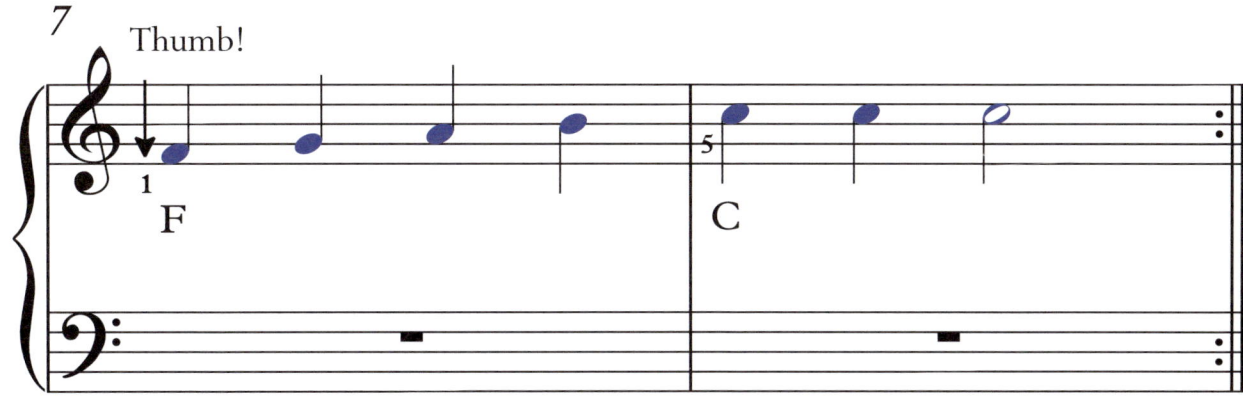

More Theory Time!
Treble Clef notes!

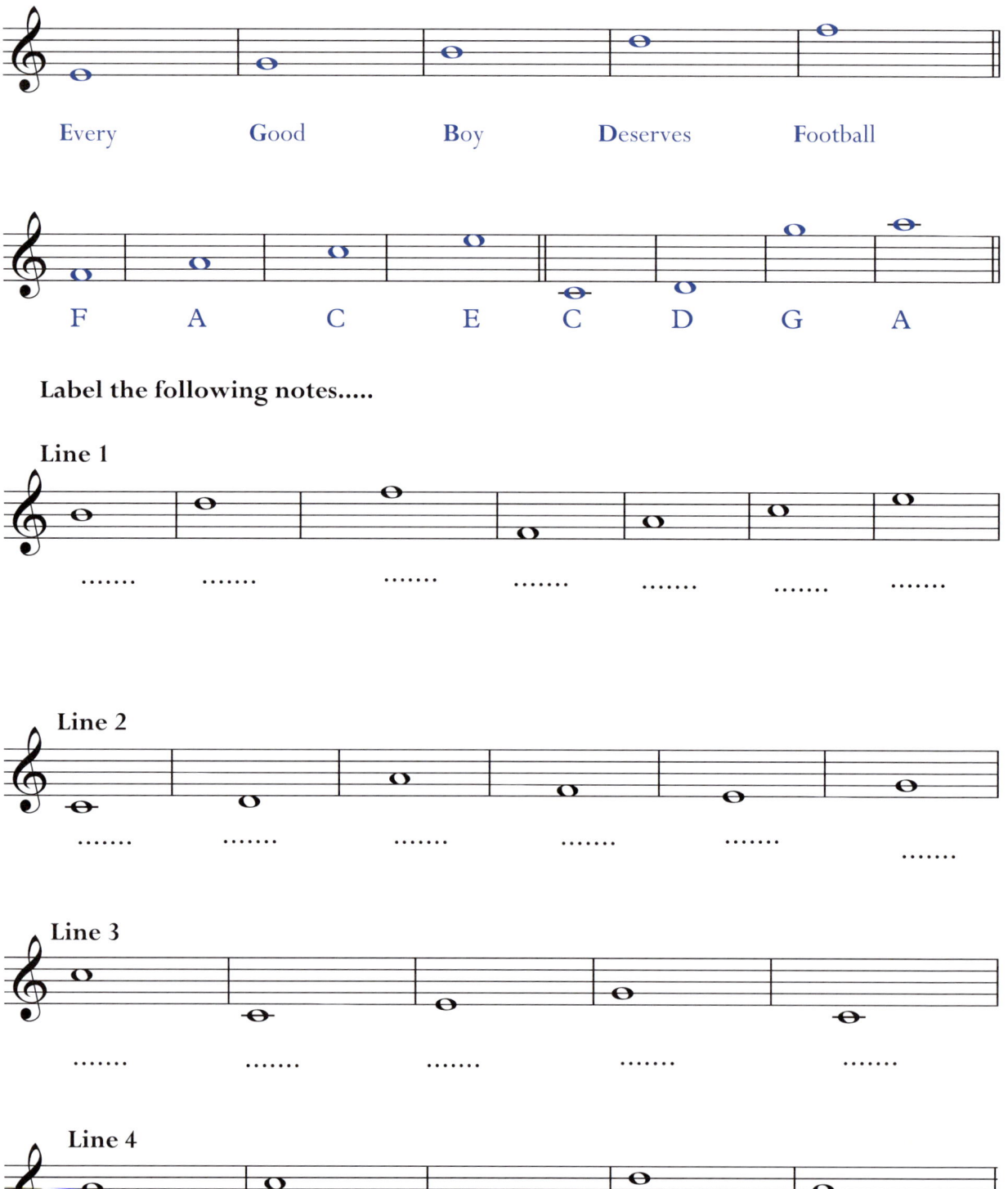

Left Hand Steps Down!

New Hand Positions!

1st Finger (thumb) begins on C,
then moves to B, then A and G

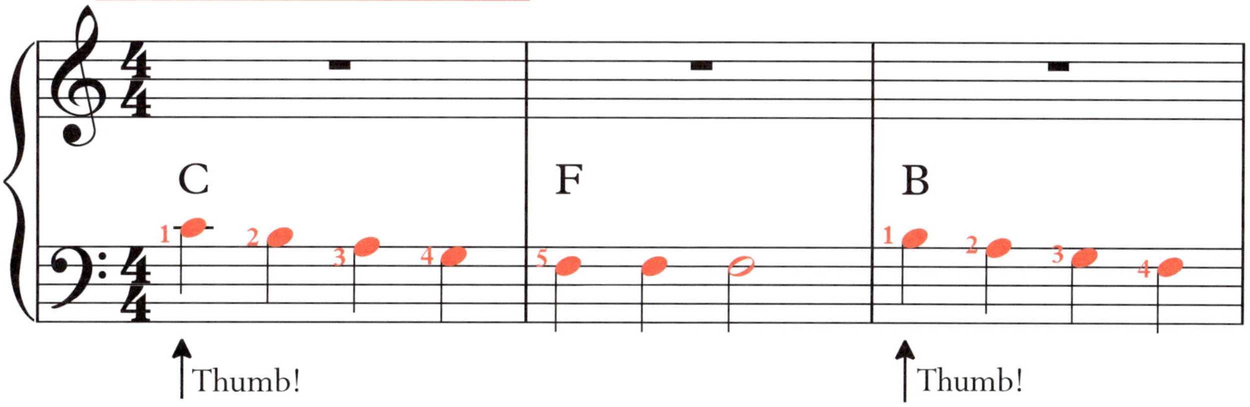

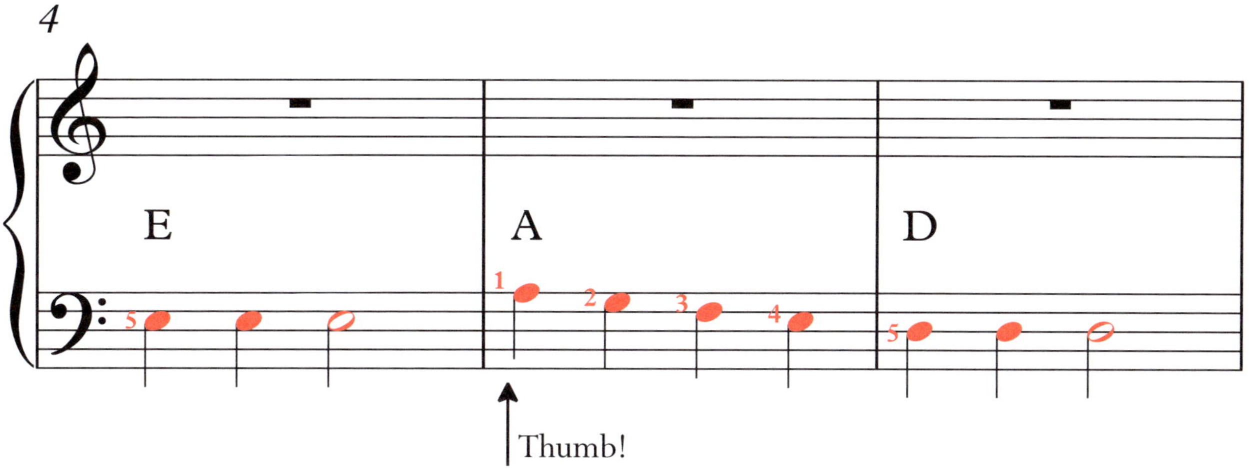

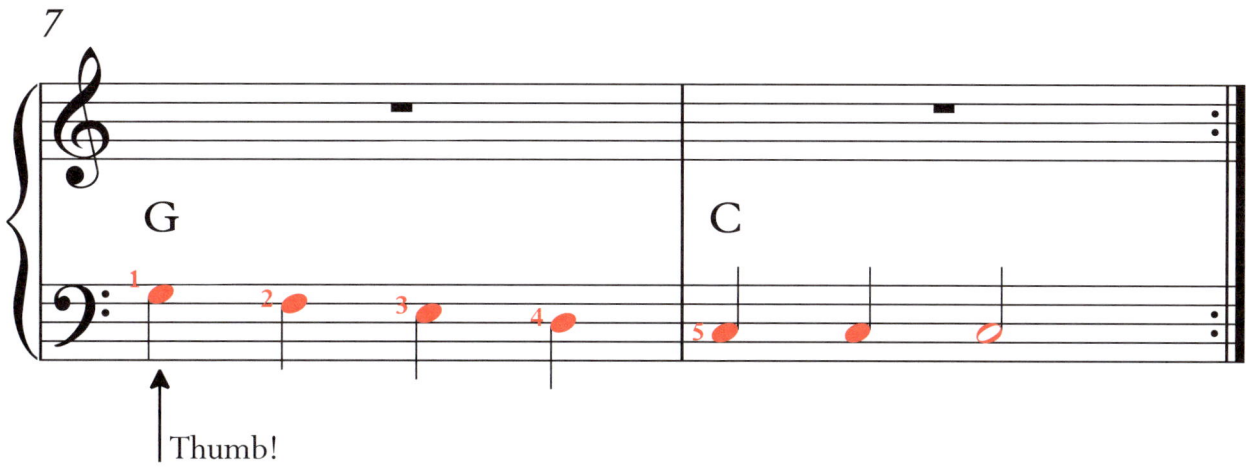

Branching Out in 4/4

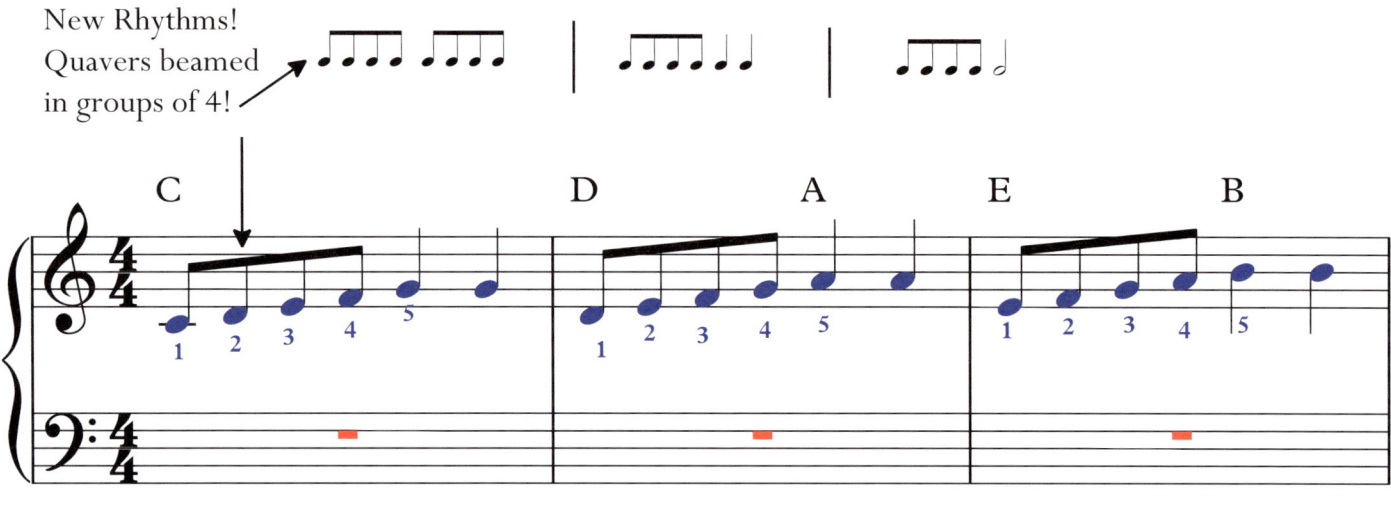
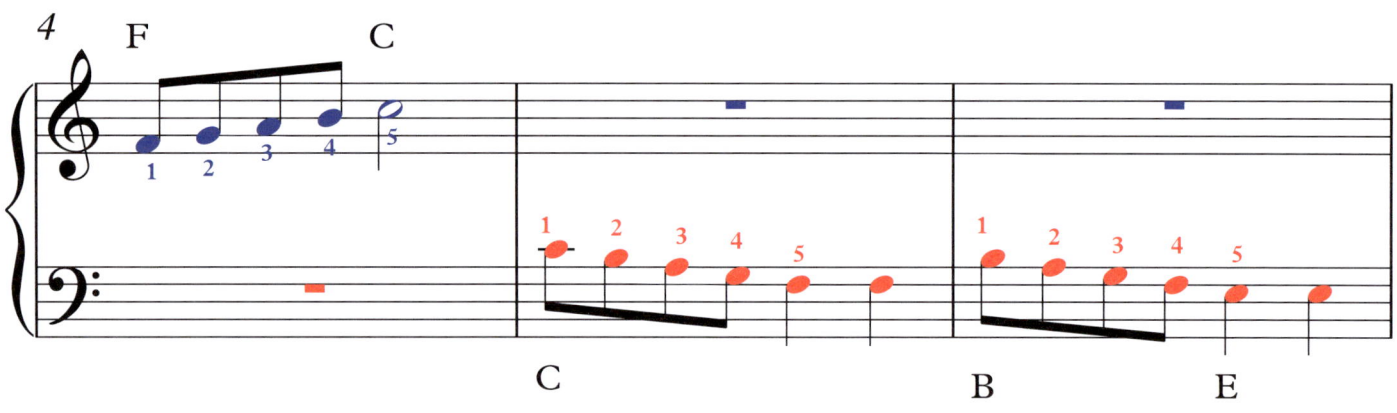
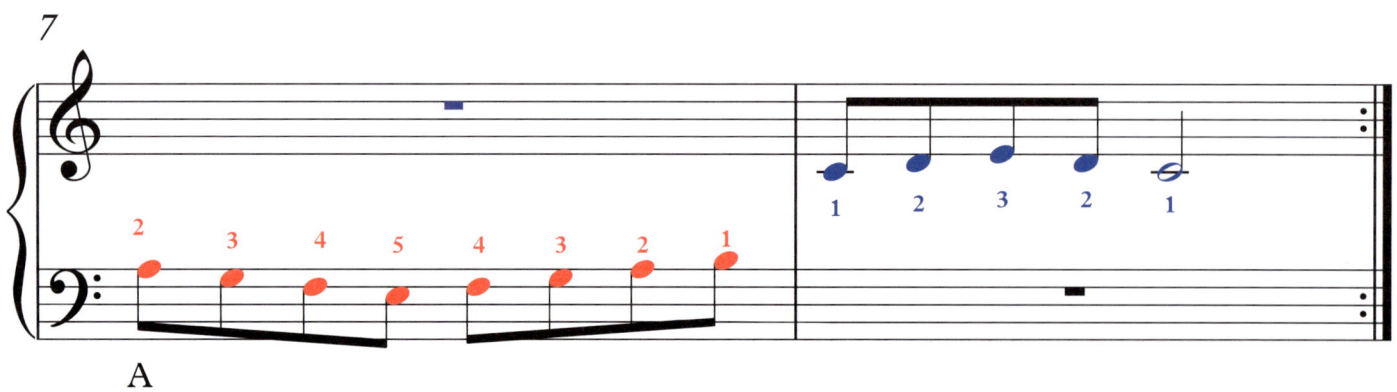

Simply Bass Clef Notes! Theory!

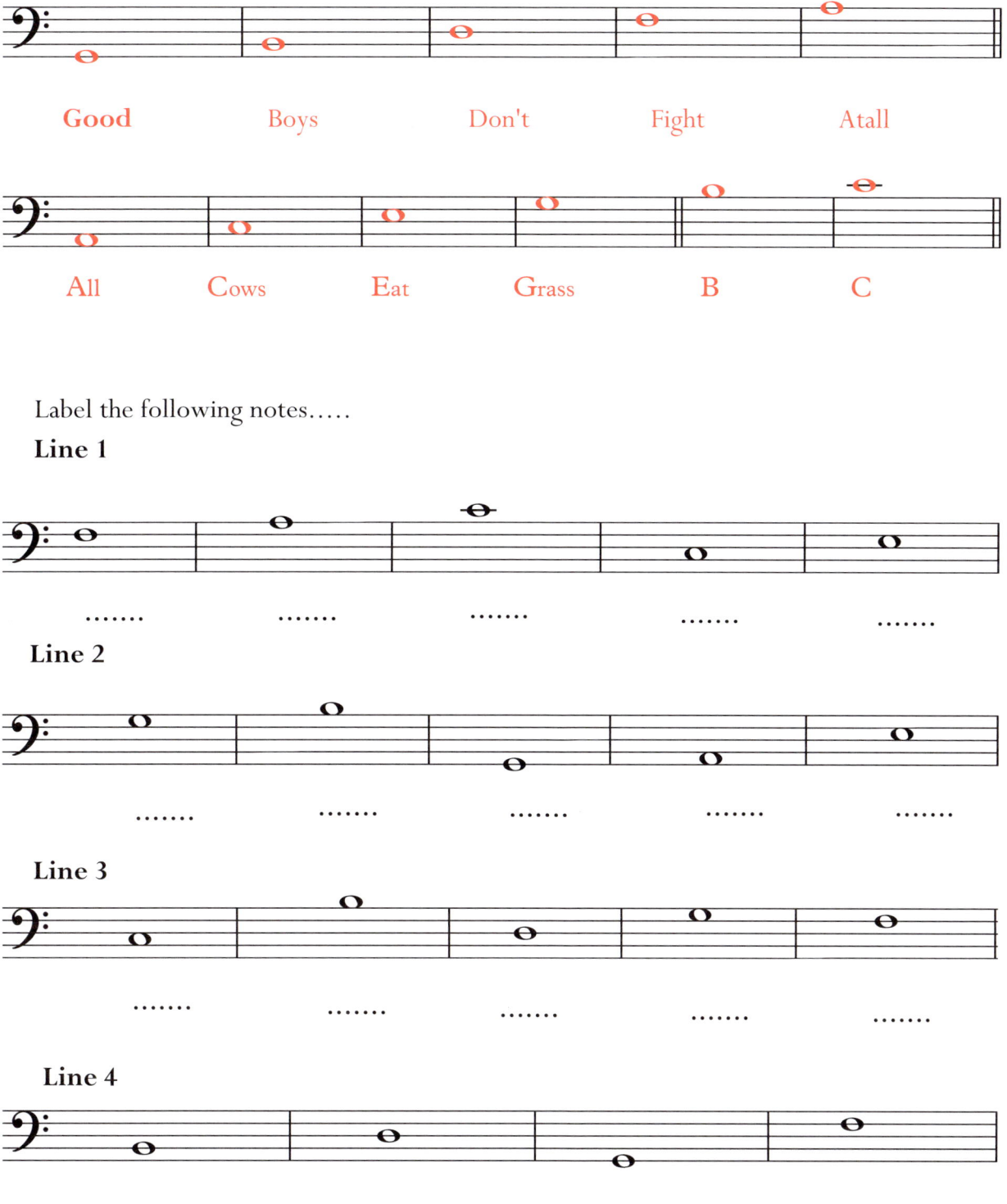

Simply Hands Together Now!
Both Thumbs Share Middle C

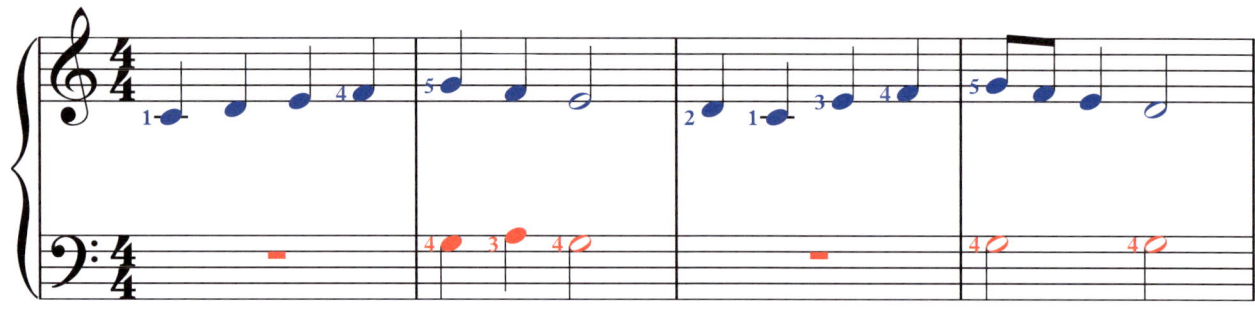

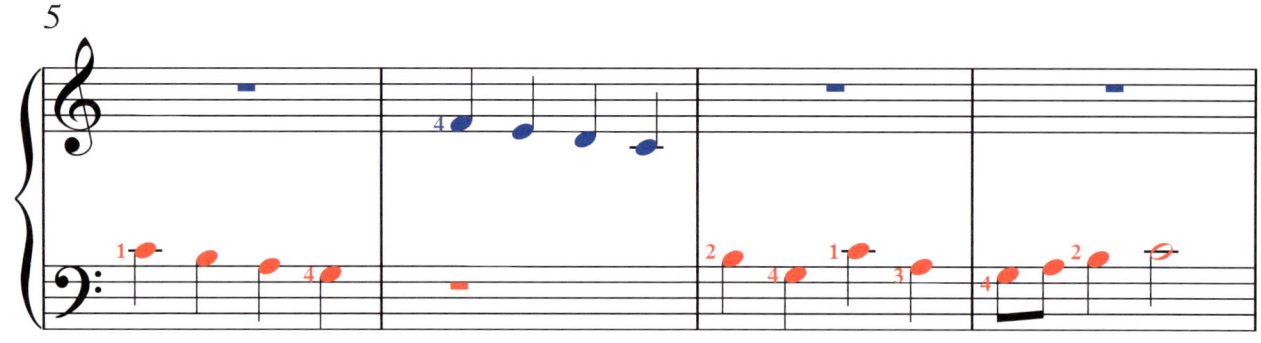

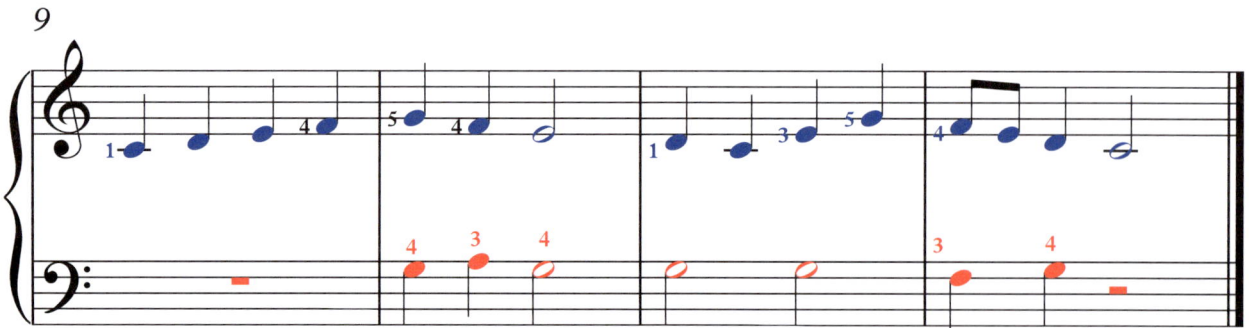

Simply 3 Beats!
Including Left Hand Chords!

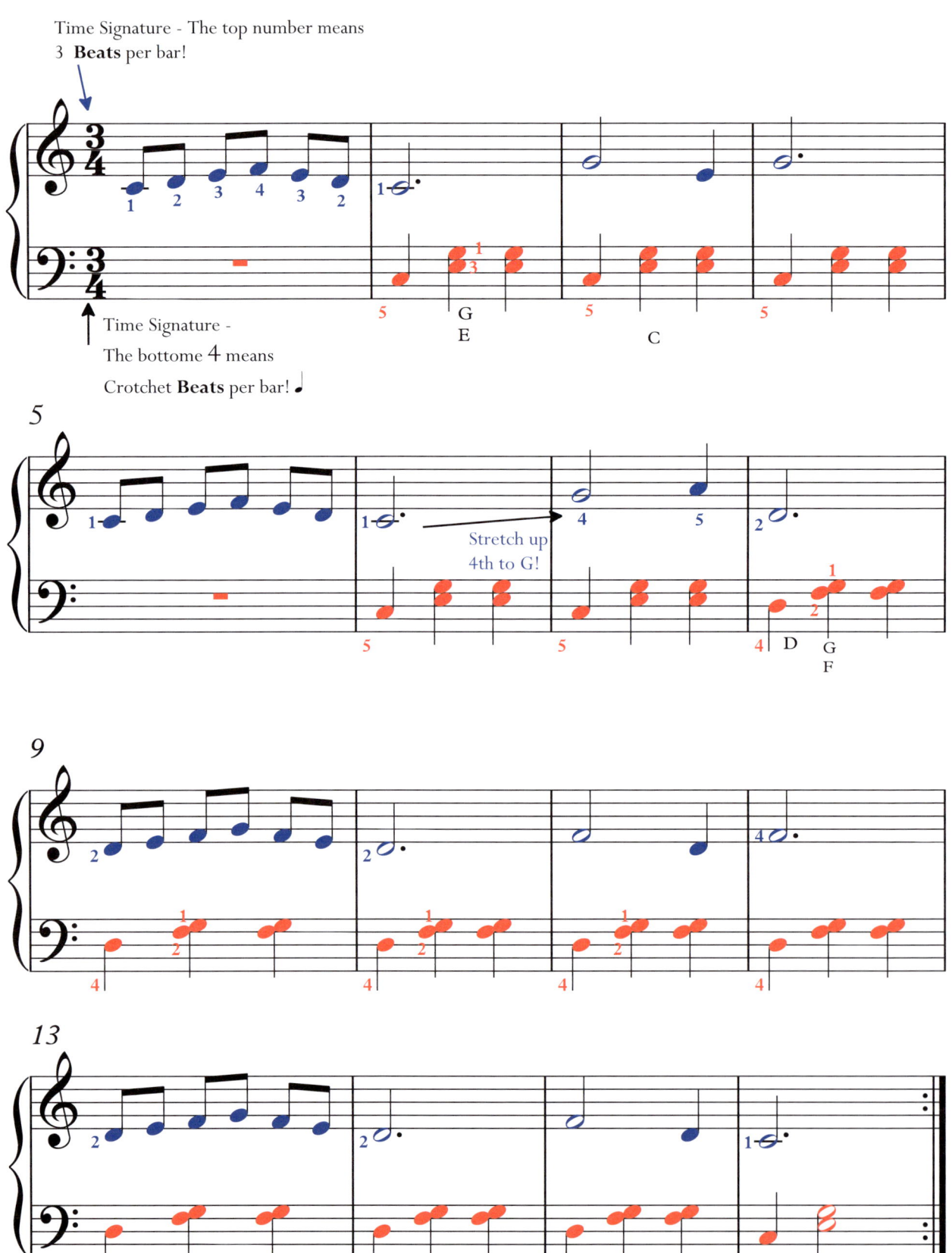

Simply a Variation

Introducing Left Hand Broken Chords!

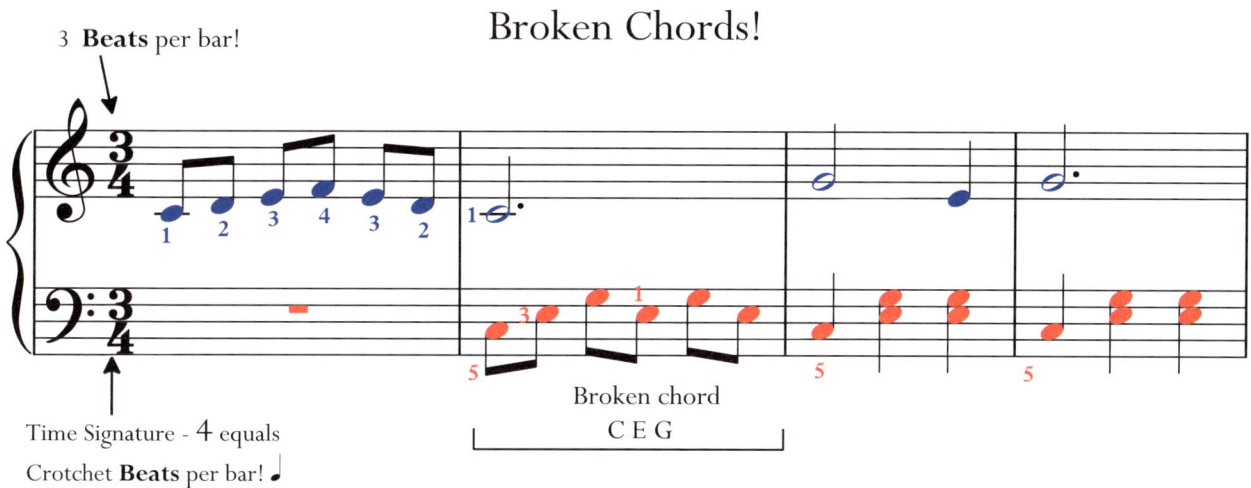

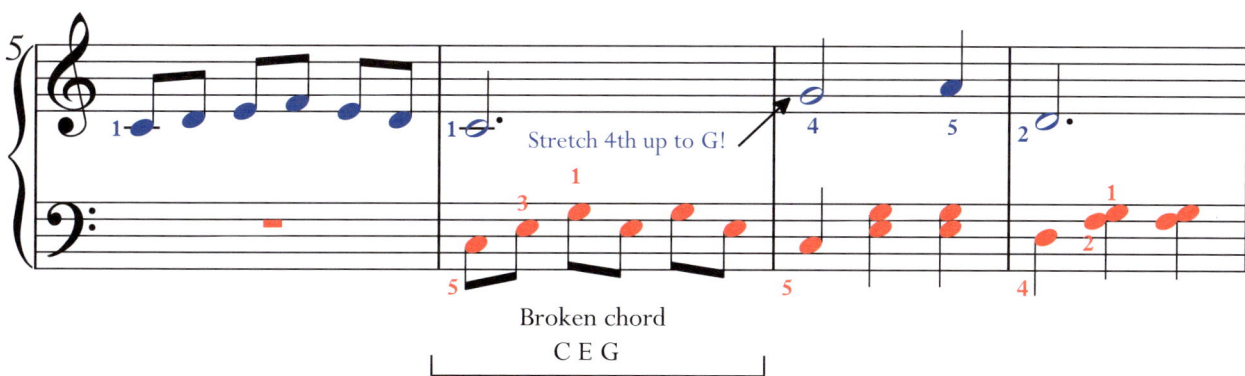

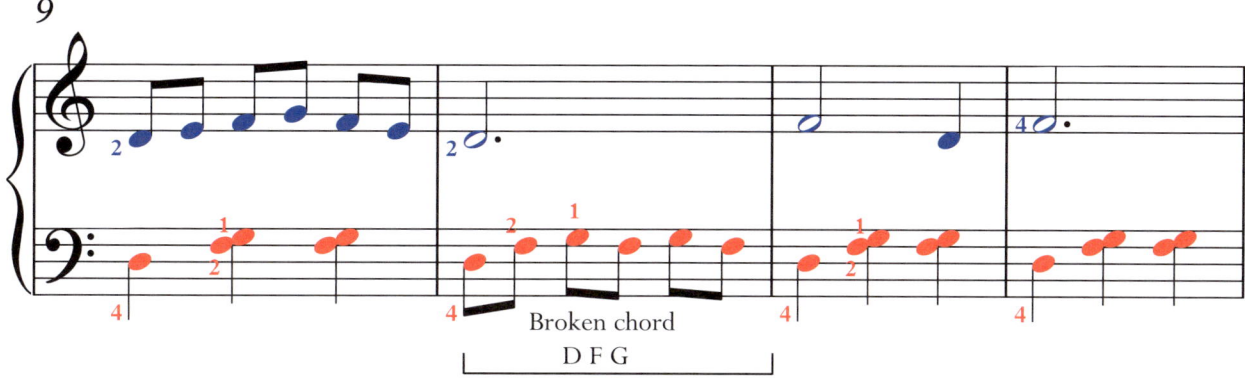

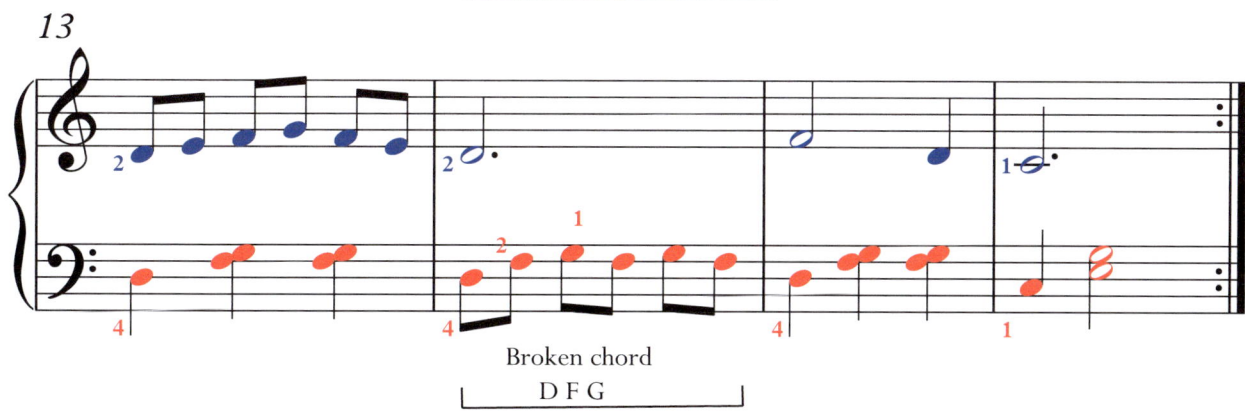

Time to Move on!

C Major Scale & Broken Chords

Before you begin....
* Find the scale passages.
* Look at the crossover fingering bars 5,6,13,14
* Look for the C major Broken chords (C E G)

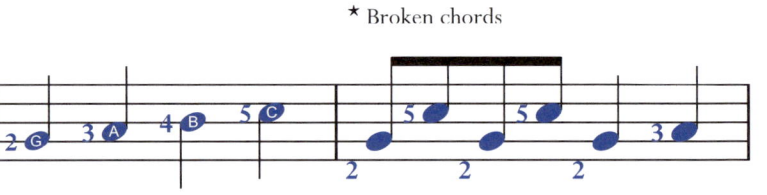
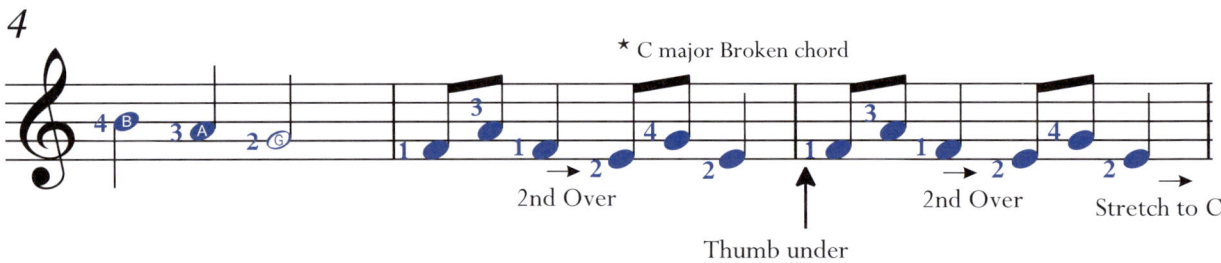
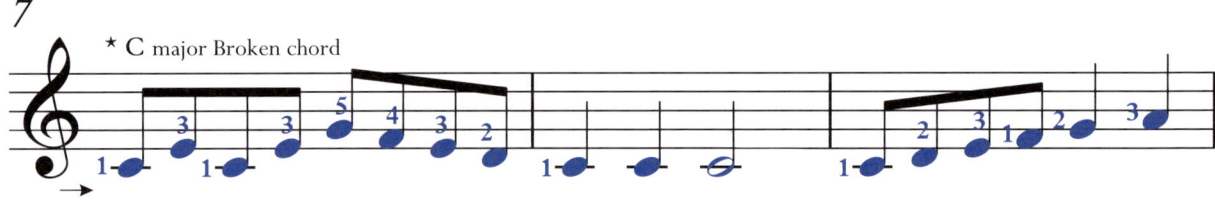

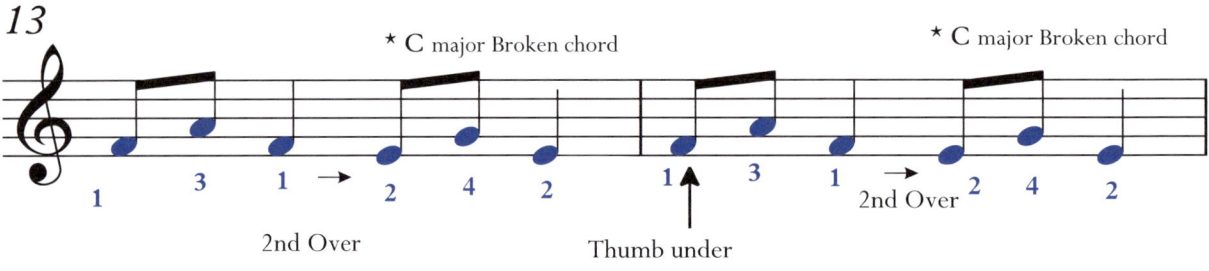
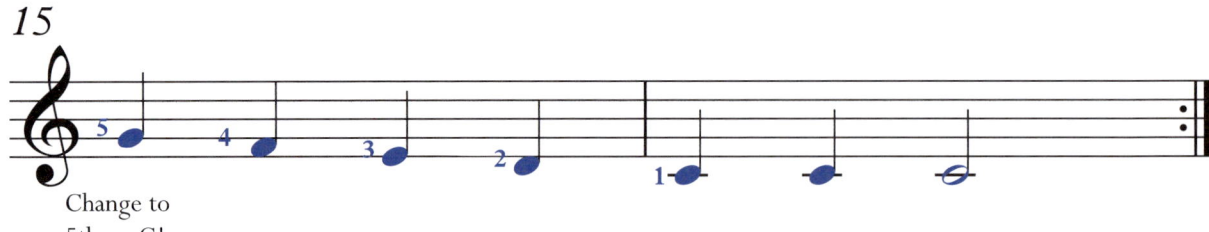

Time to Sharpen Up!

G Major Scale In Crotchets!

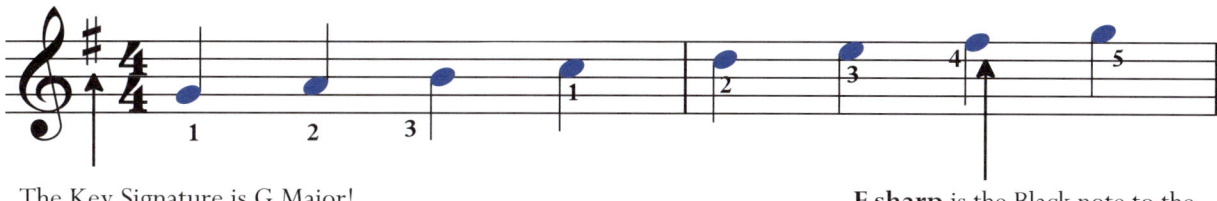

The Key Signature is G Major!
G major has an F#, which means that all F's should be played as sharps!

F sharp is the Black note to the **Right of F** on the Piano!

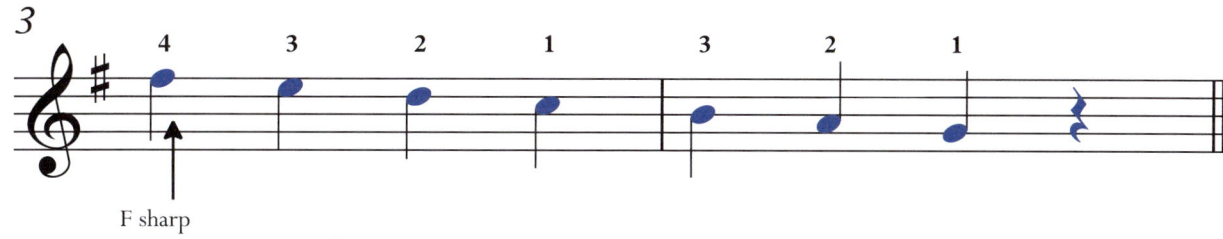

F sharp

The G Major Study In Quavers!

Stretch thumb to 5th for Top G

G major ascending & descending!

G major descending!

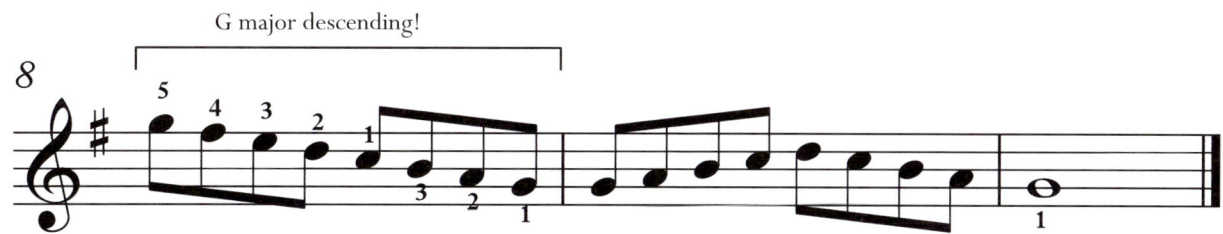

The Echo
Transposed!

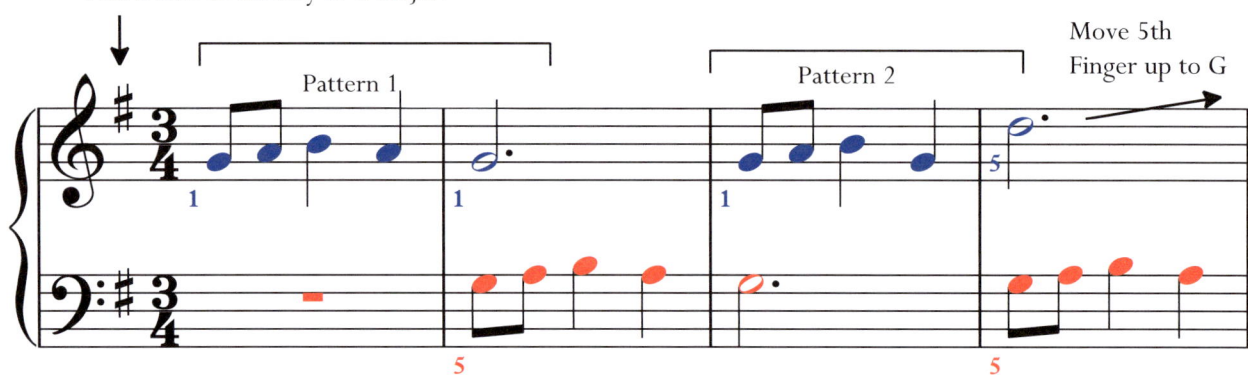
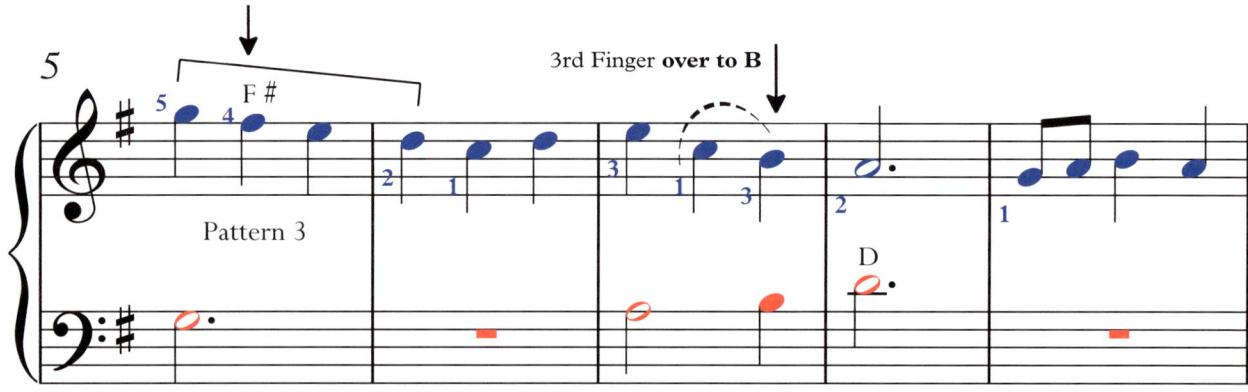
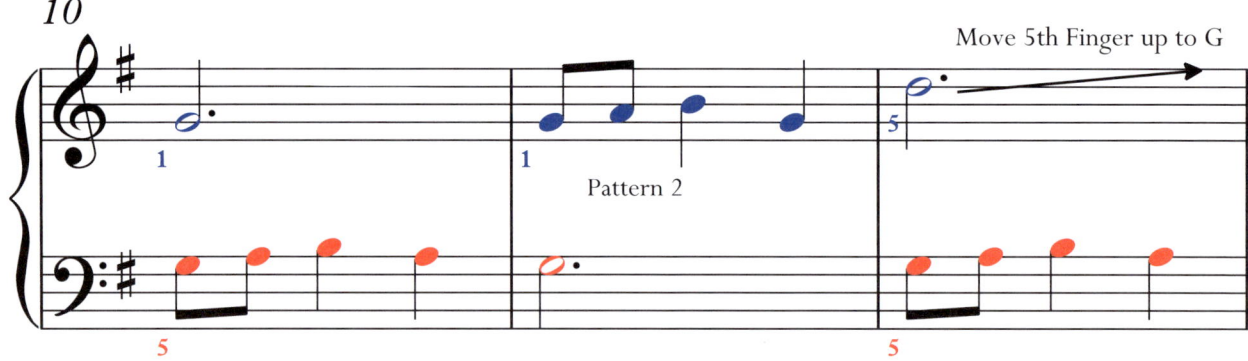
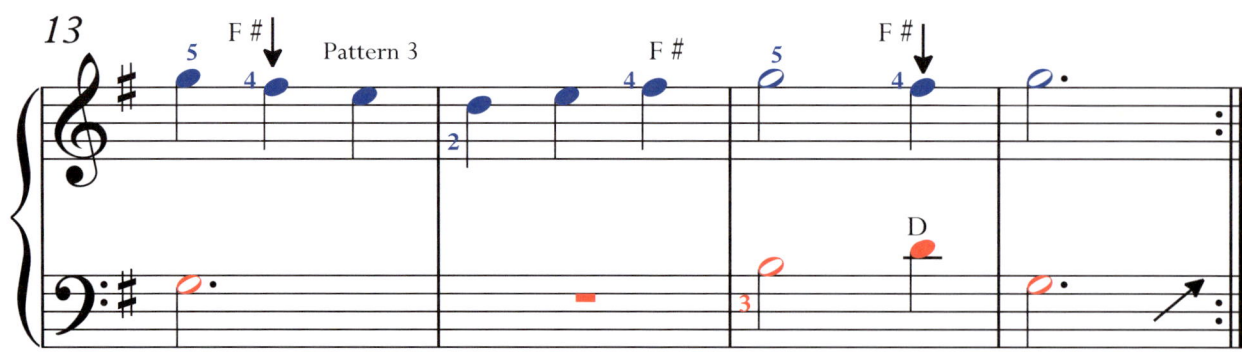

Repeat!

Right Hand Scales
Beginning on D!

D Major Scale On 8ve

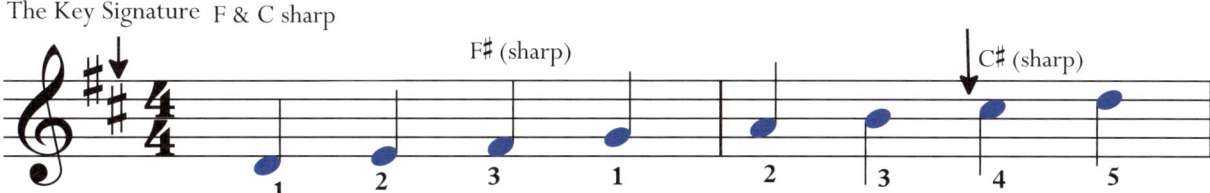

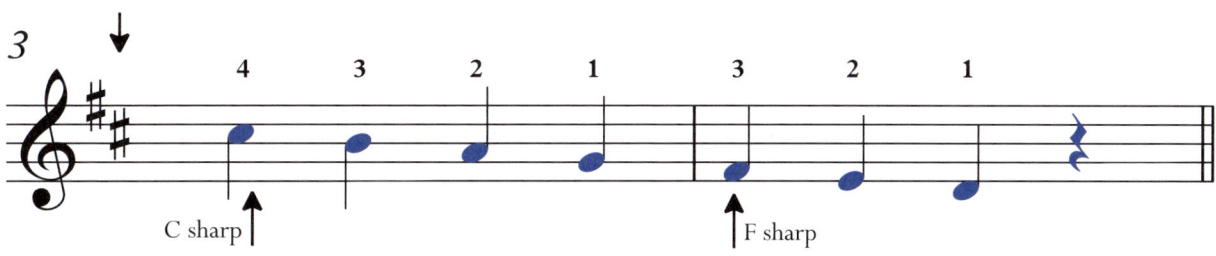

D Chromatic scale one 8ve!

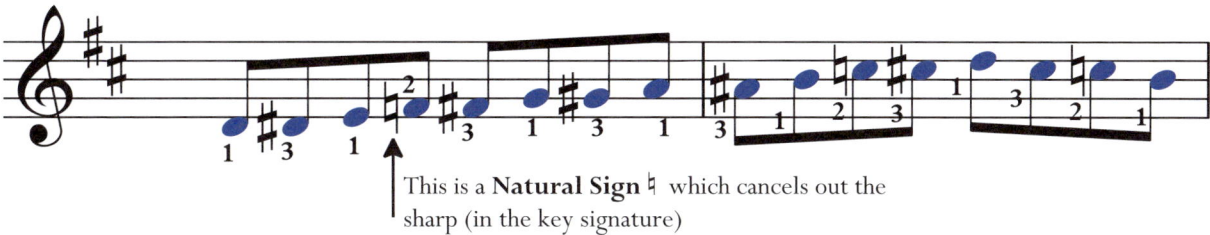

Chromatic movement - going up or down in semitones!
D Chromatic scale is moving up and down in semitones!

Remember to use 1st & 2nd fingers on the white keys & 3rd on the black keys!

The
Snake Charmer

Includes The Chromatic Scale!

Composer Joanne Fairclough

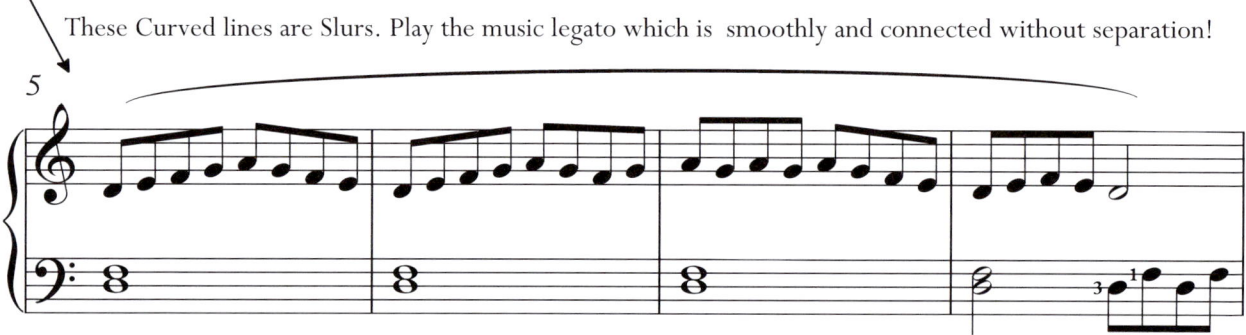

These Curved lines are Slurs. Play the music legato which is smoothly and connected without separation!

*Slurs indicate Legato!
Legato means smooth and connected!

Minor to Major!

E Minor Right Hand One 8ve

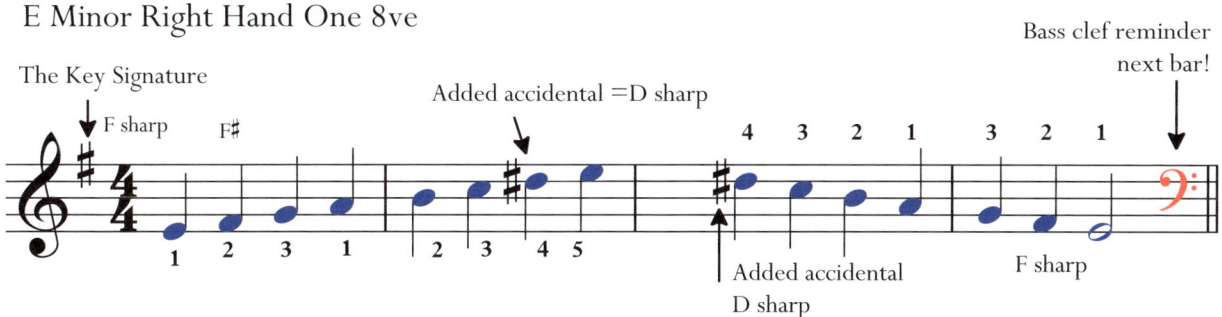

* In E Minor, Sharpen the 7th degree of the scale from D to D sharp!

E Minor Left Hand One 8ve

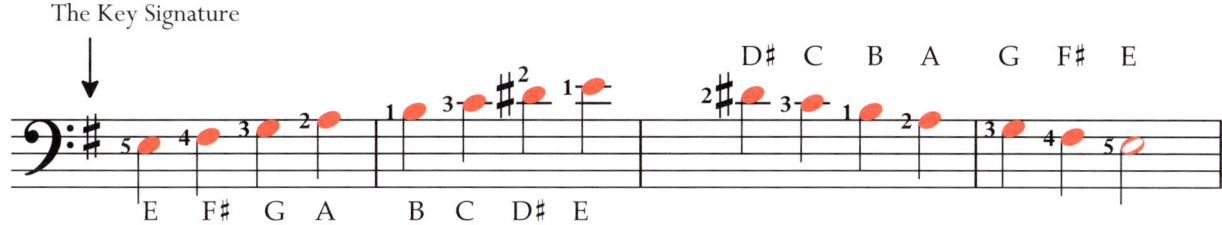

* E Minor & G Major Share the Same Key Signature of F♯

G Major Left Hand One 8ve

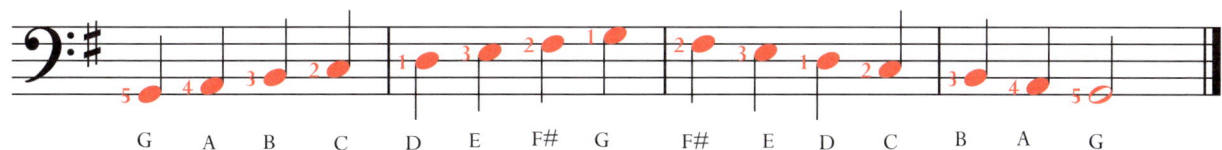

Broken Chord Study
With Left hand Extension!

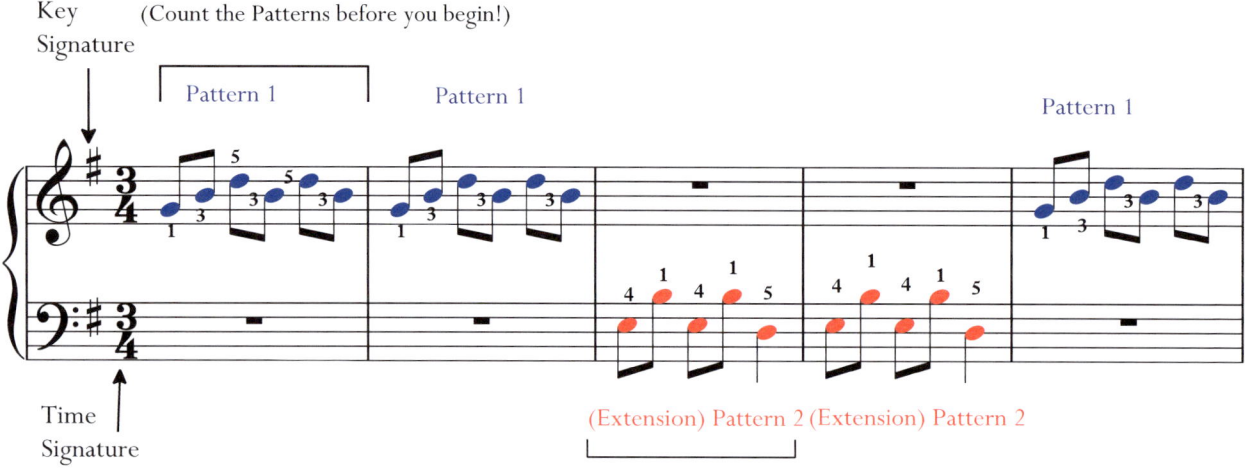

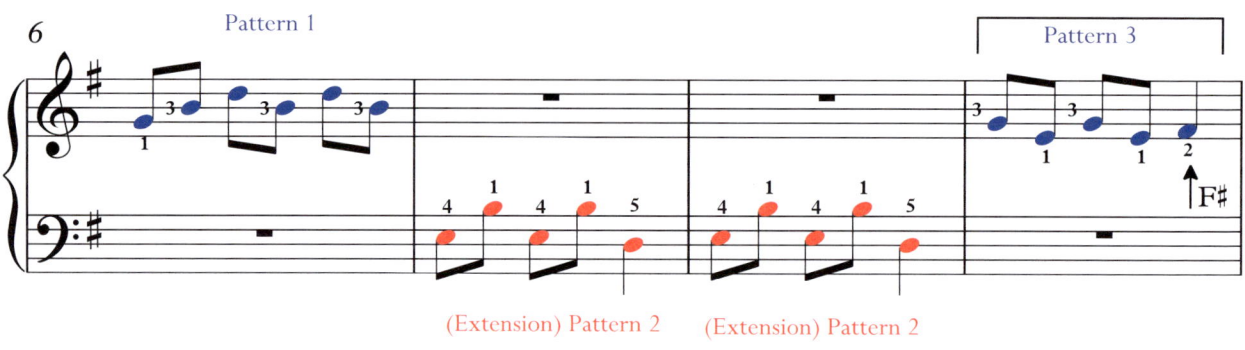

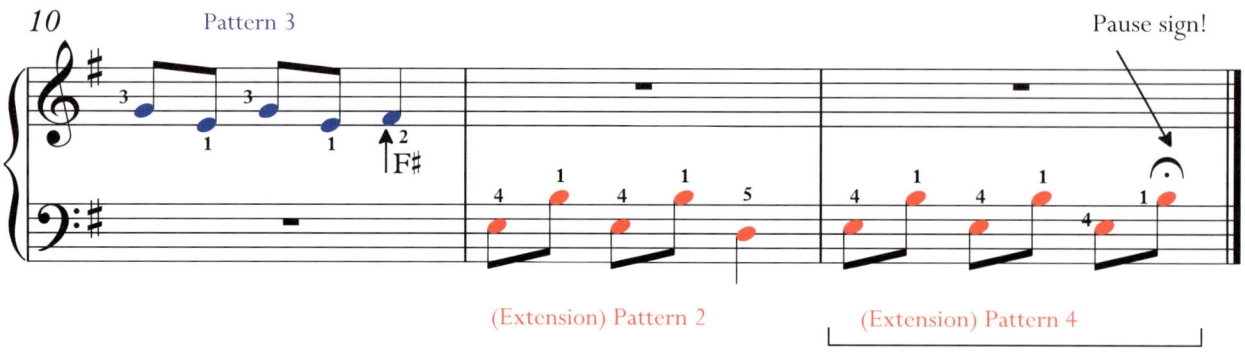

The **Pause** sign indicates to hold the note down for longer than it's value (♪)

The Music Box

Composer Joanne Fairclough

Dynamics **p** (soft) m**p** (moderately soft) **mf** (moderately loud) *rall.* (Gradually slow down)

More Scales!
Together now in Similar Motion!

F Major Scale One 8ve

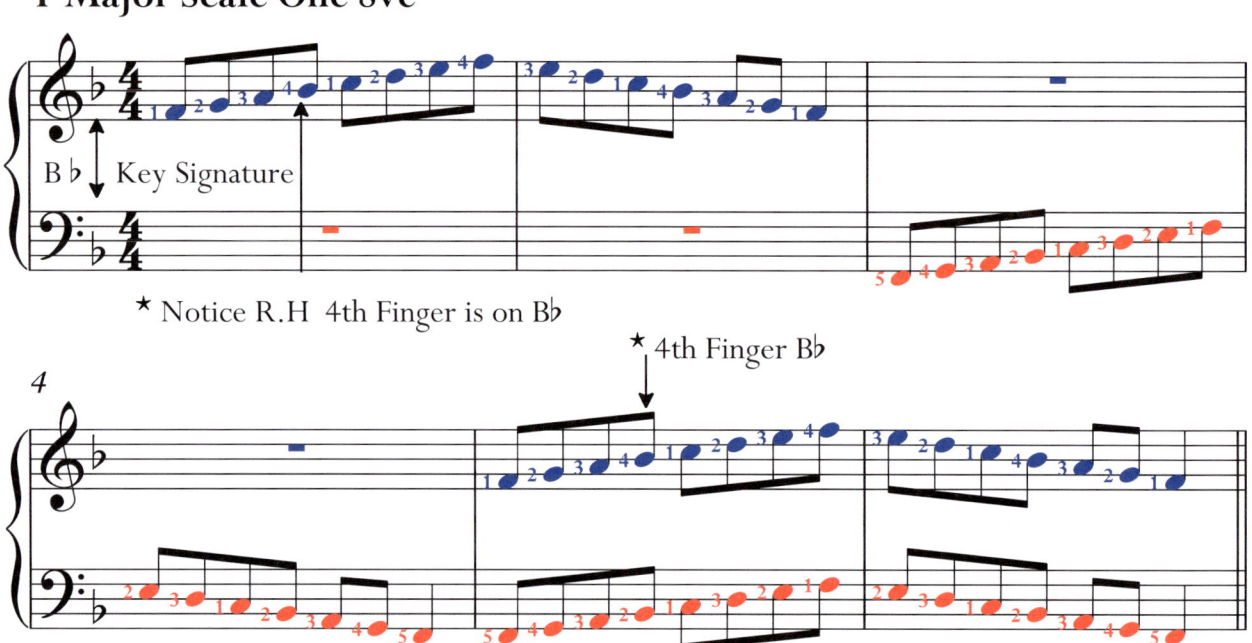

★ Notice R.H 4th Finger is on B♭

★ 4th Finger B♭

D Harmonic Minor Scale One 8ve

★ Notice the added accidental C♯

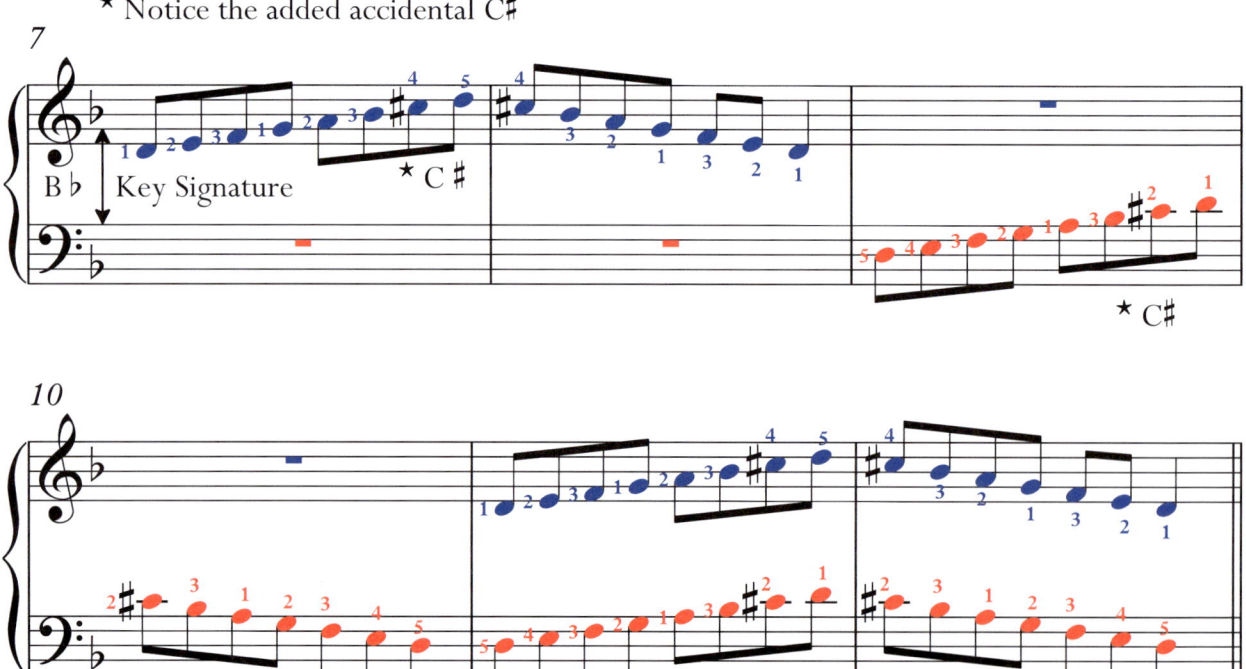

More Bass Clef Theory!
Including Leger Lines⋆!
(⋆The little extra lines above & below the stave!)

The **Stave** consists of
5 Lines & 4 Spaces!

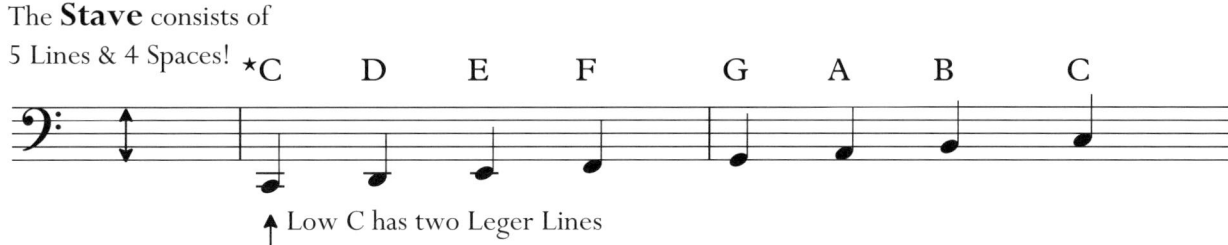

↑ Low C has two Leger Lines
Below the stave

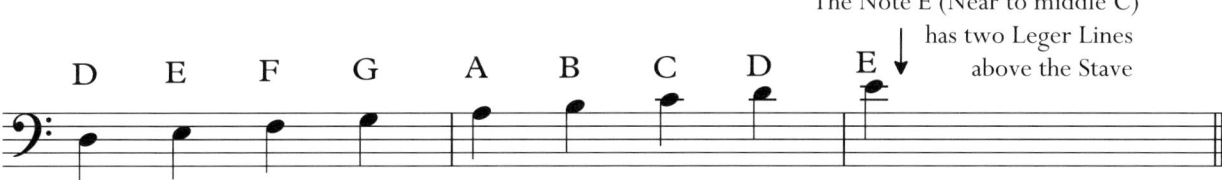

The Note E (Near to middle C)
has two Leger Lines
above the Stave

⋆ Sharp ♯ Raises the note by a semi-tone

1. Name the following Notes (include the sharp signs)

……… ……… ……… ……… ……… ……… ……… ……… ………

2. Name the following Notes

……… ……… ……… ……… ……… ……… ……… ………

⋆ Flat ♭ lowers the note by a semi-tone

3. Name the following Notes including the flat signs:

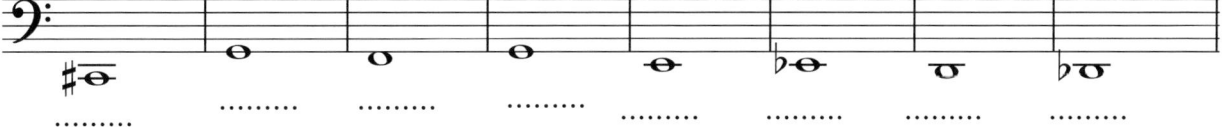

……… ……… ……… ……… ……… ……… ……… ………

A Variation on Chords!
Left Hand Only!

Variation 1- Block Triad Chords

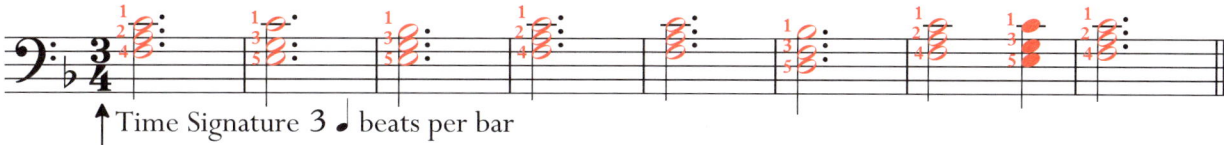

↑Time Signature 3 ♩ beats per bar

Variation 2 - Block Chords in 3rds

Variation 3 - Broken Chords in crotchets

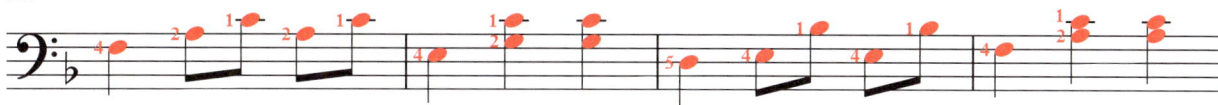

Variation 4 - Broken Chords with added quavers

↑The Key Signature is B Flat (B♭) Notice that the flat symbol is on the 2nd line up!
The Key of this piece is F Major.

A Theme & Variation on
Happy Birthday To You!

Let's Rock The Boat!

Leap Frog!
Introduction to Intervals!

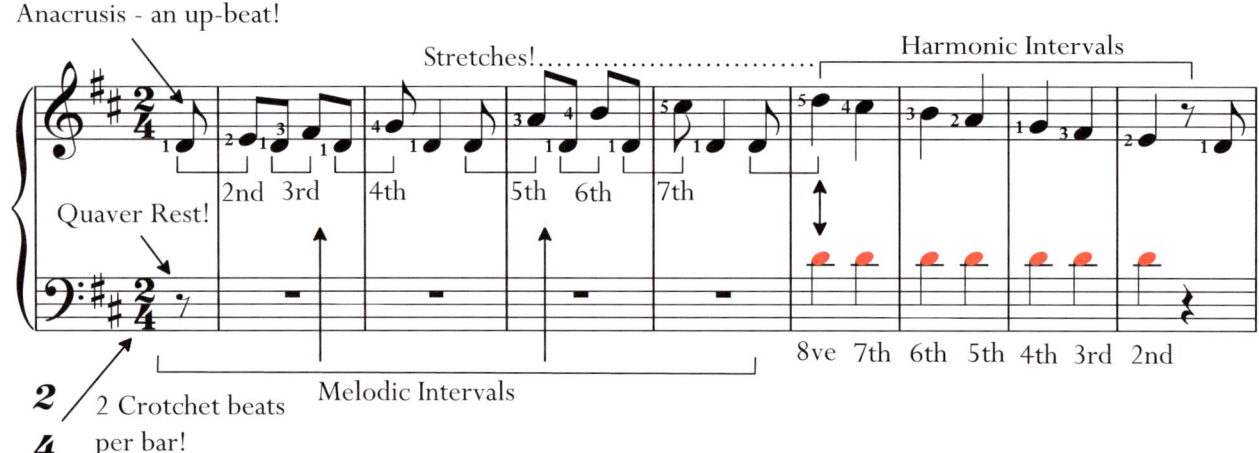

Name the following **melodic** intervals.

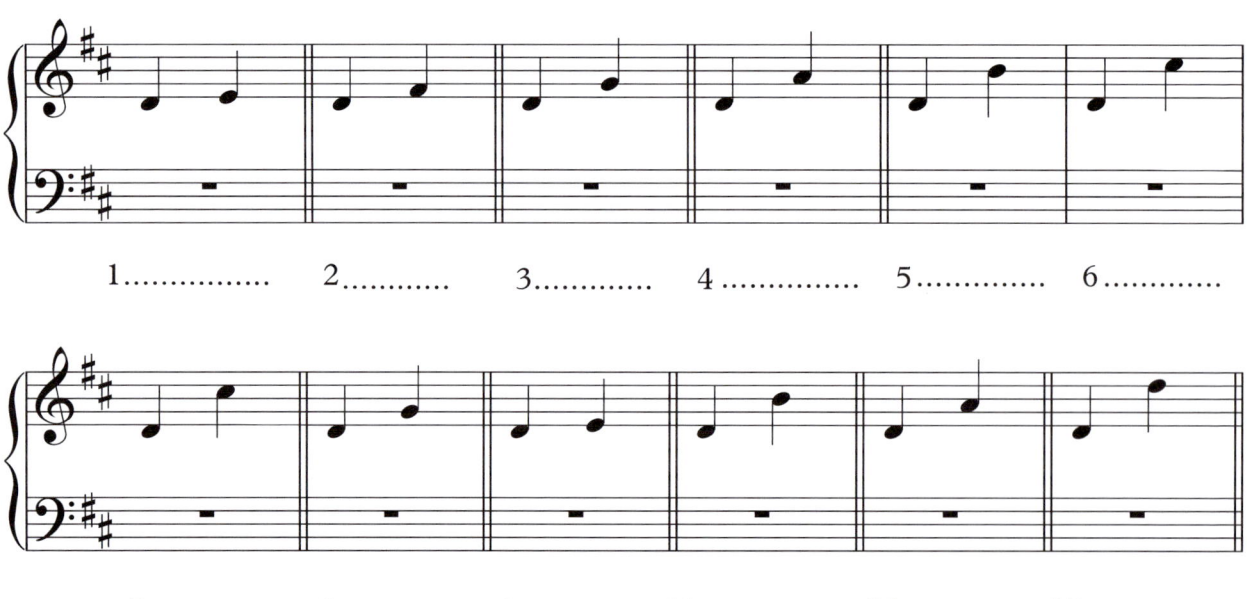

Harmonic Intervals -
Two notes played together, creating harmony!

Melodic Intervals
These make a melody!

Anacrusis - an up-beat!
(Not beginning on the 1st beat of the bar)

Simply Basic Blues!
Walking Bass & Chromaticism!

Chromaticism is moving up or down in semitones!
A semitone is half a tone which is one step up or down to the nearest note on the keyboard!

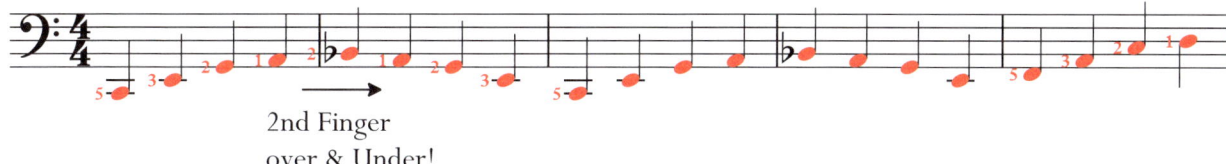

2nd Finger over & Under!

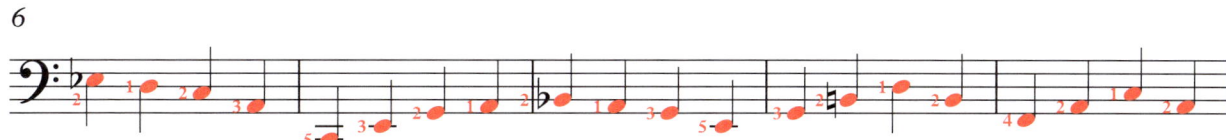

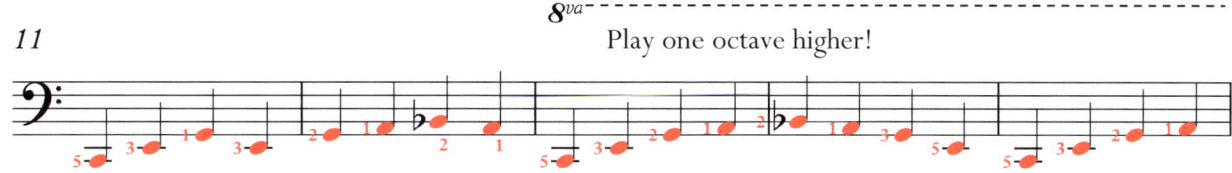

Play one octave higher!

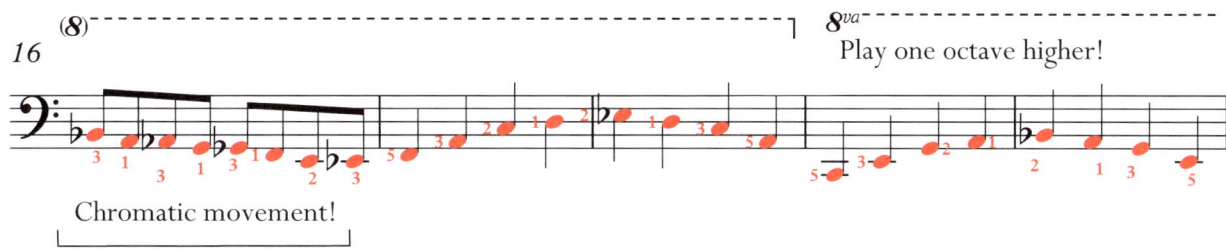

Chromatic movement!

Play one octave higher!

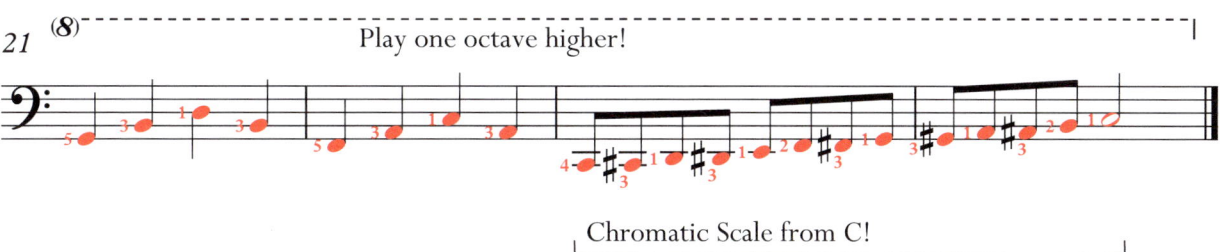

Play one octave higher!

Chromatic Scale from C!

Developing Rhythms in a Scale Study!

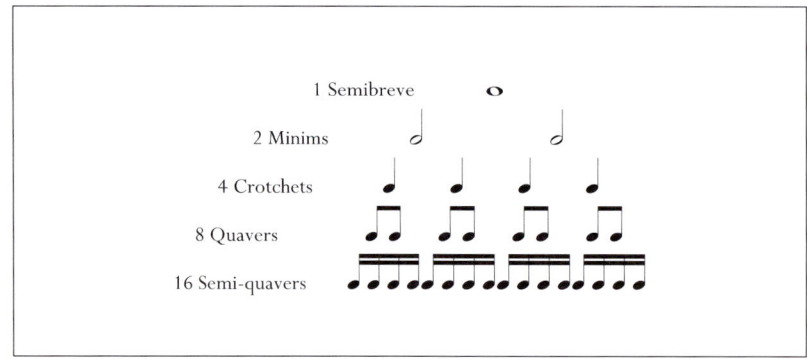

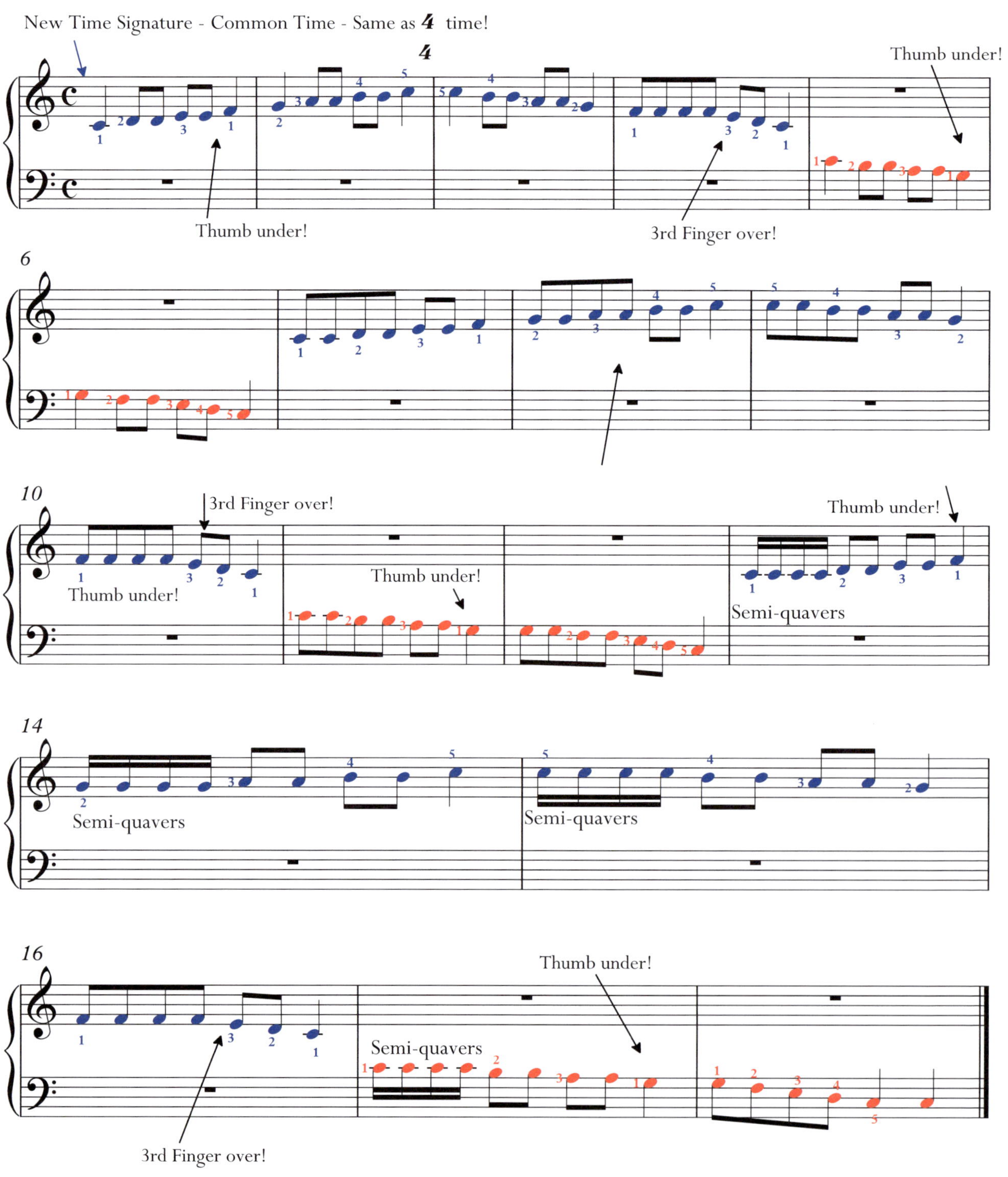

The Robin!

New Rhythm
Dotted Crotchet & quaver

Composer Joanne Fairclough

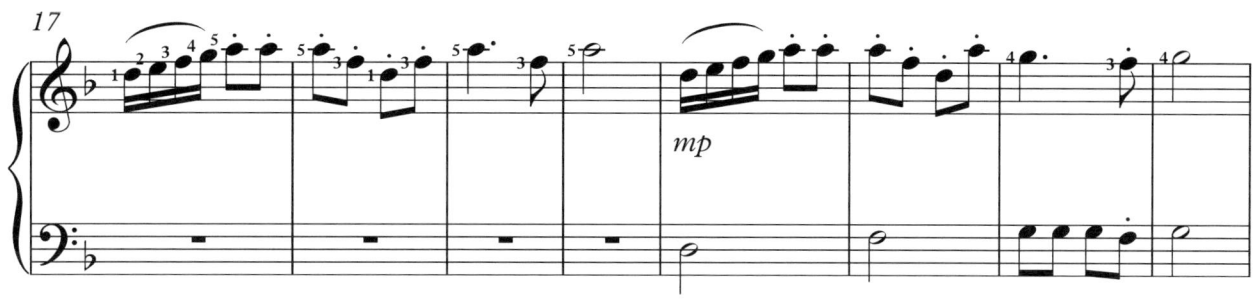

Time to Study Arpegios!

Arpegios are notes taken from a chord and
then arranged in ascending or descending order …
In this study the notes are from the C Major Chord!

For the One octave arpegio fingering …be aware of the stretches!

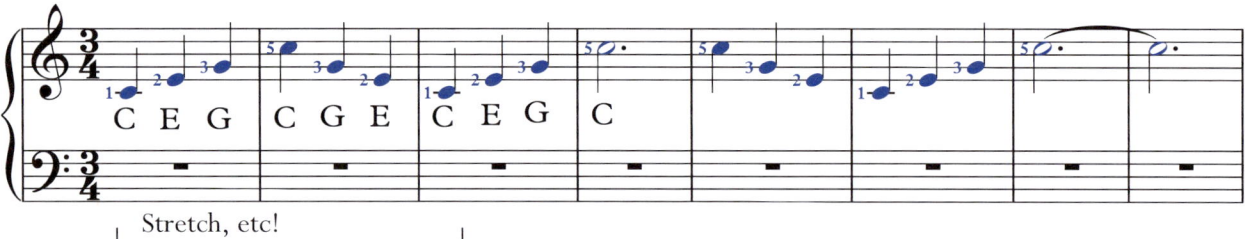

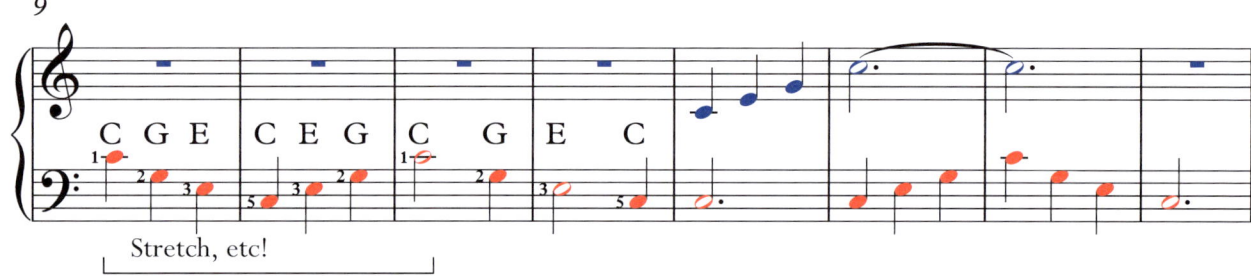

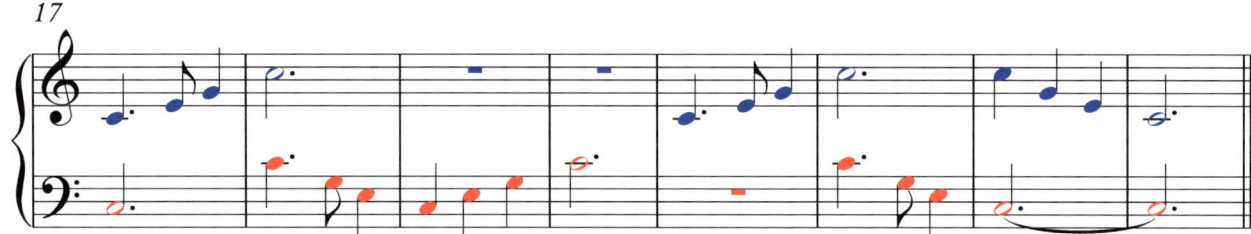

Extension Study - Arpegios in 2 octaves …be thumbs under & 3rd fingers over!

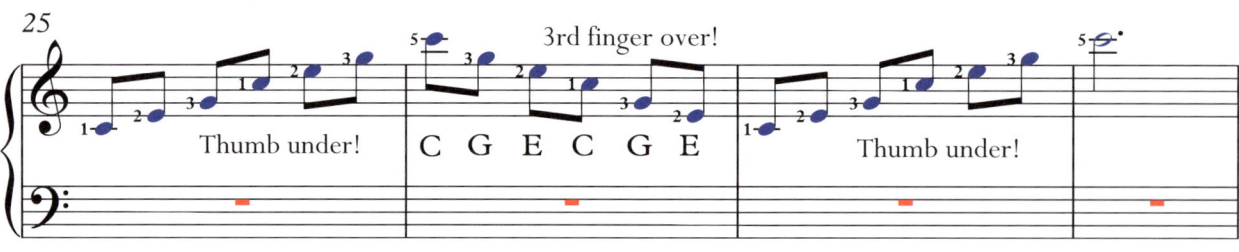

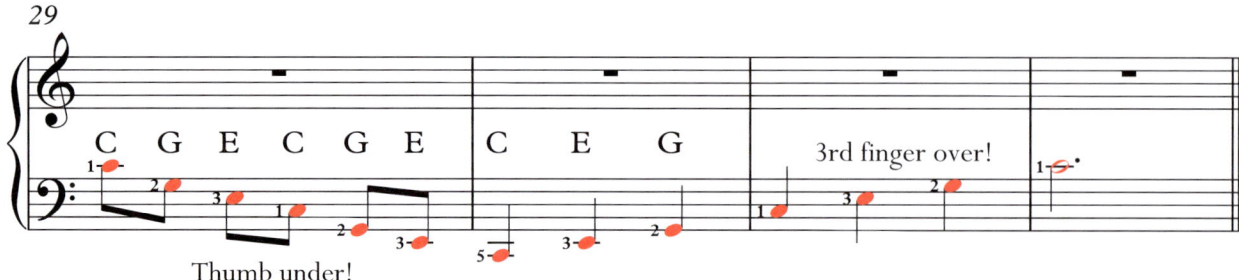

Octave Leaps!
(8 Note Leaps)

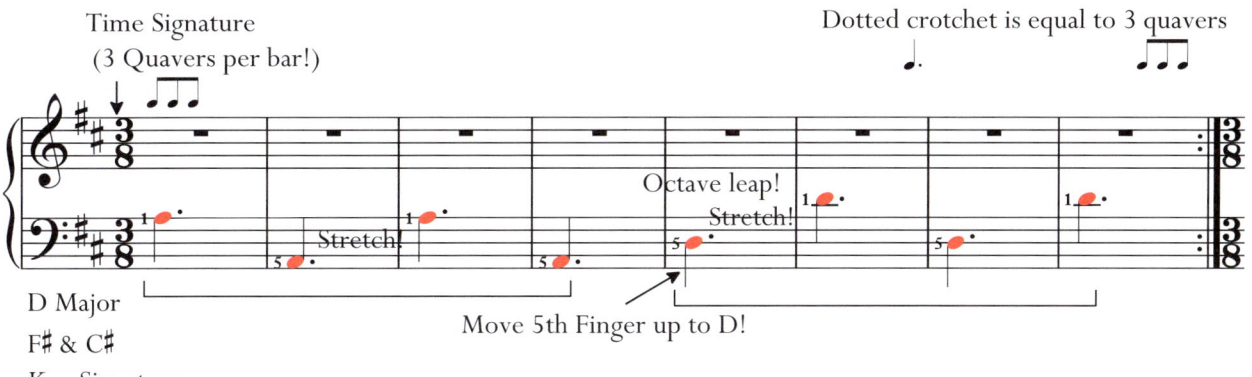

D Major
F# & C#
Key Signature

The Swinging Hammock!

Joanne Fairclough

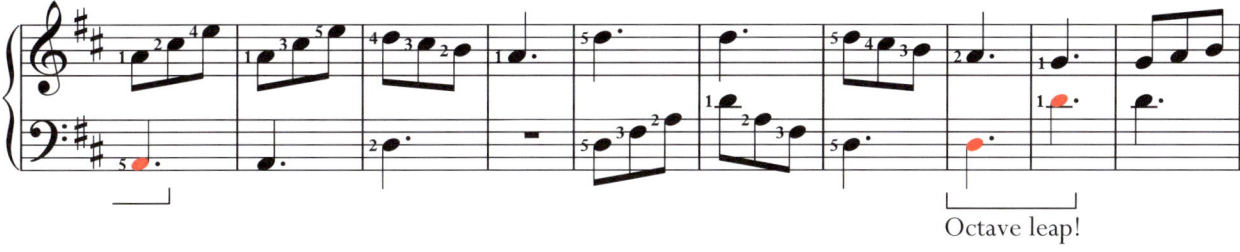

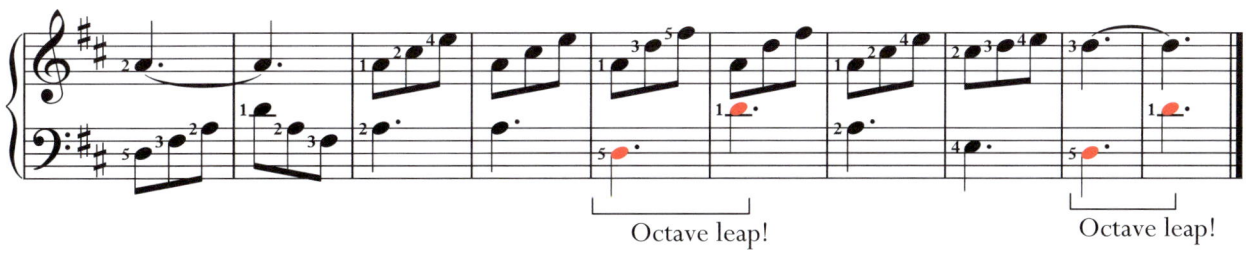

Simply Add Clefs!

Draw the Treble or Bass Clef in front of the following notes!

As an example, the treble clef has been added in front of the first note…
(N.B. If a bass clef was added before this note, it would have been an E!),

Line 1

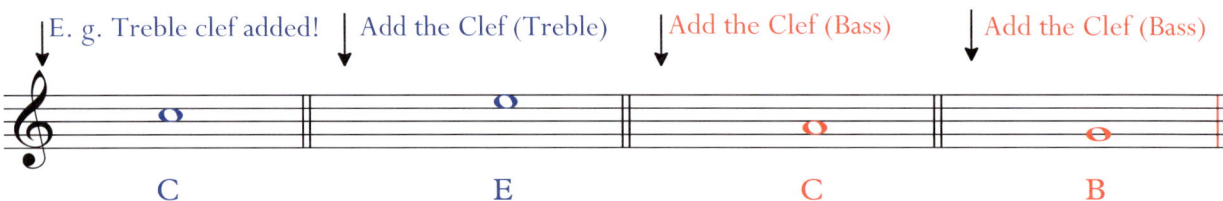

Line 2

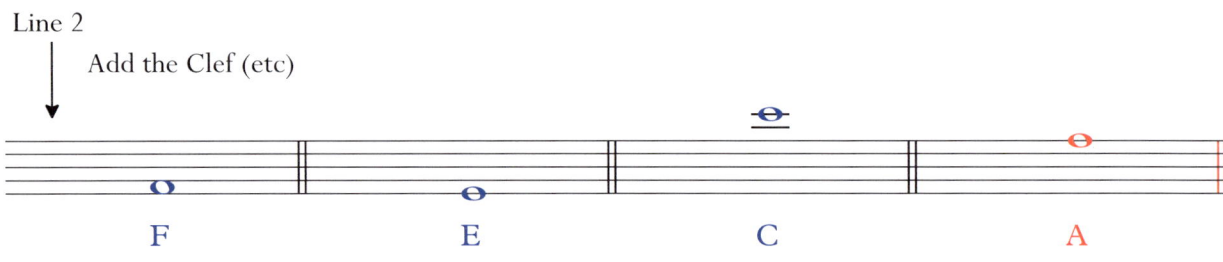

Line 3

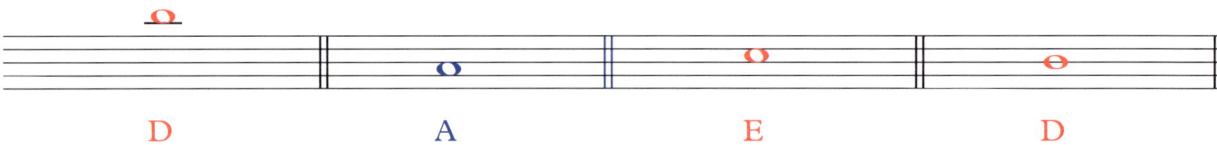

Line 4

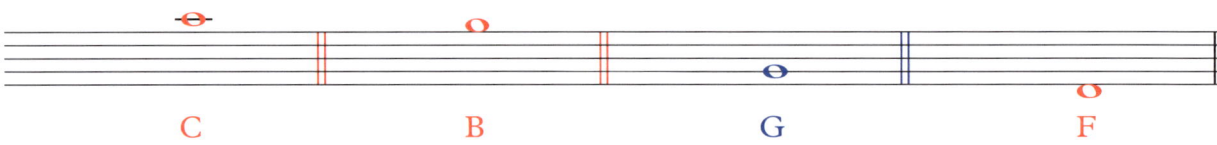

Line 5

Sci-Fi!
Triplet Study

 = ♩
3 Quaver triplets are equal to one Crotchet beat!

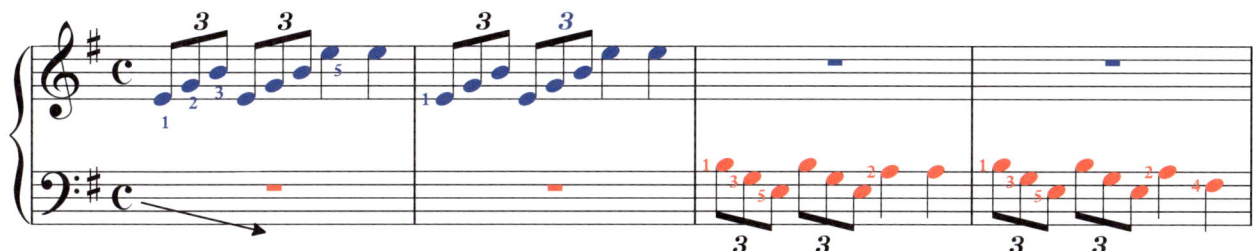

Time Signature is **C**

which has the same meaning as **4/4**

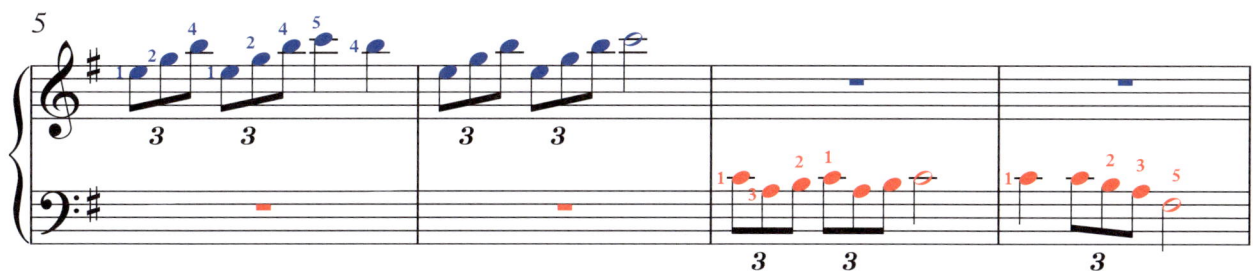

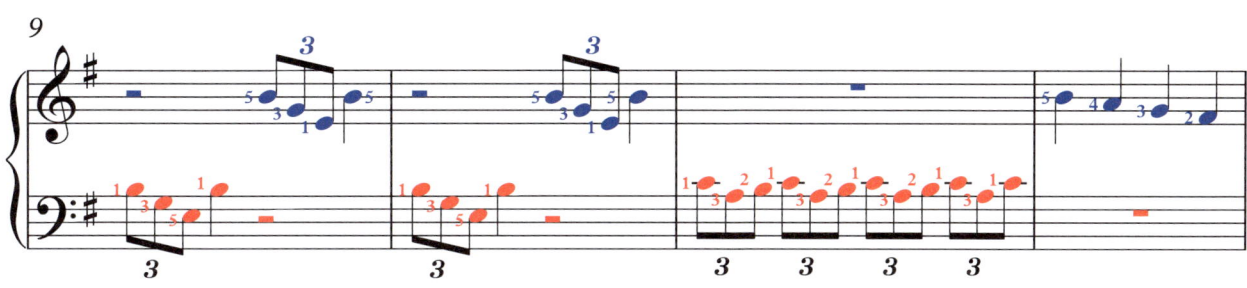

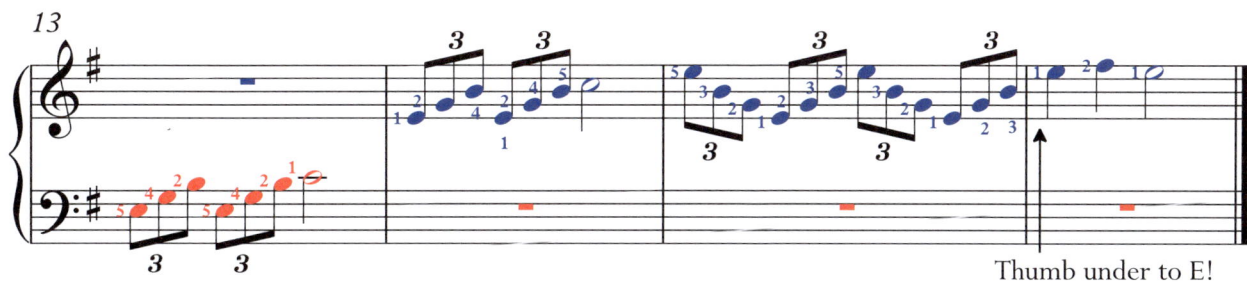

Thumb under to E!

Let's Harp On!

This piece is in the Key of E Minor!
E Minor has added accidentals C♯ & D♯

Moderato - Dolce

Composer Joanne Fairclough

Time Signature is **C** for Common Time
(4 Beats per bar!)

1st & 2nd Fingers over & under!

1st Finger under!

1st & 2nd Fingers over & under!

pp *very soft* **p** *soft* **mp** *moderately soft* **mf** *moderately loud* ────── *gradually getting quieter*

Strolling Along!
Dotted Crotchet & Quaver Rhythms!

Composer Joanne Fairclough

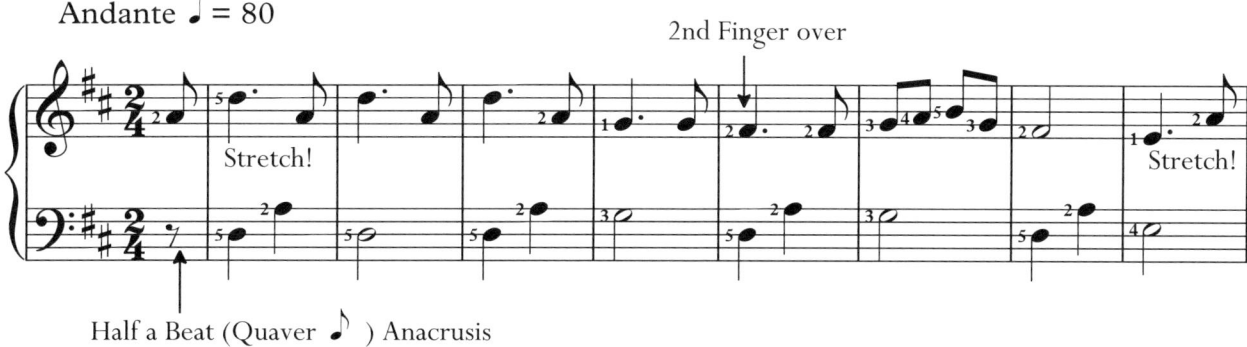

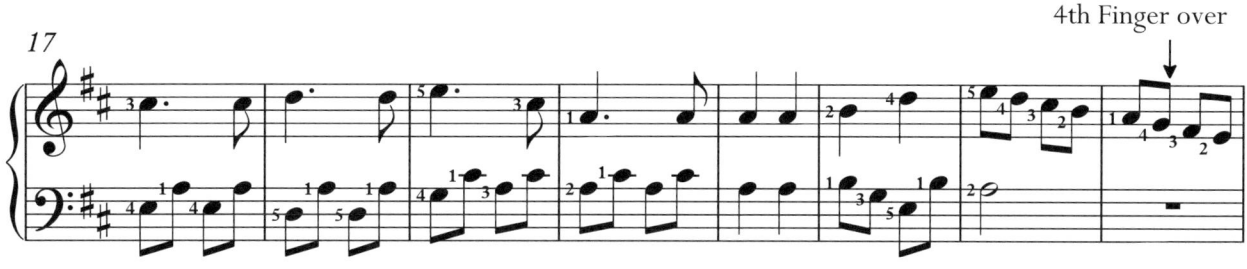

Blues Bass!

Walking Bass & Chromaticism!
Look out for the accidentals!
♭ (flats) ♯ (sharps) ♮ (naturals)

Lento - Slowly

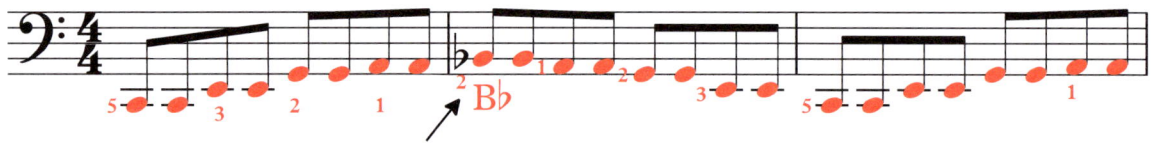

* 2nd Finger over & 1st under!

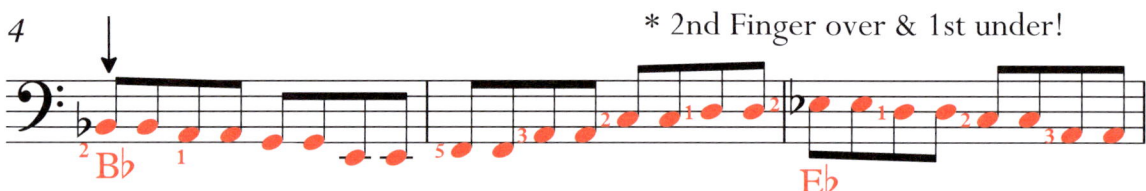

* 2nd Finger over & 1st under!

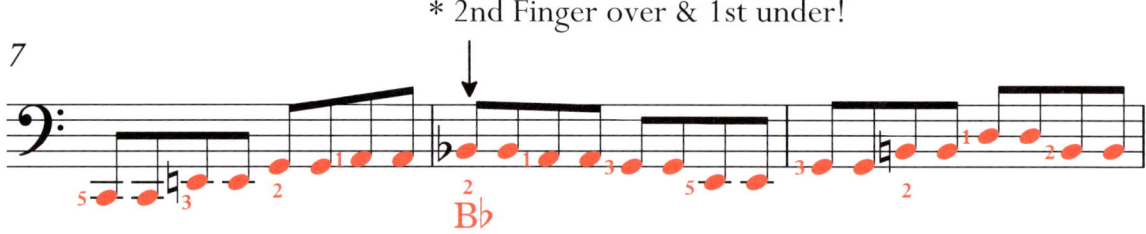

* 2nd Finger over & 1st under!

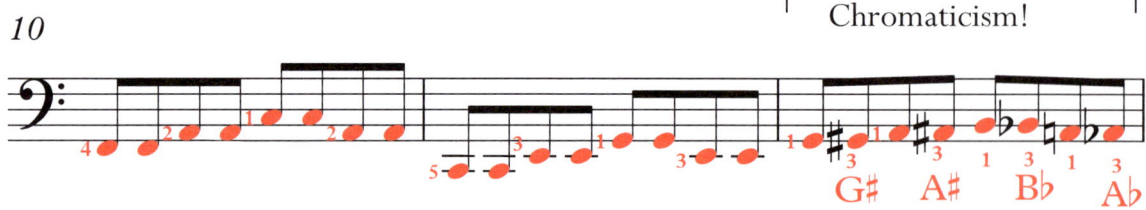

Chromaticism!

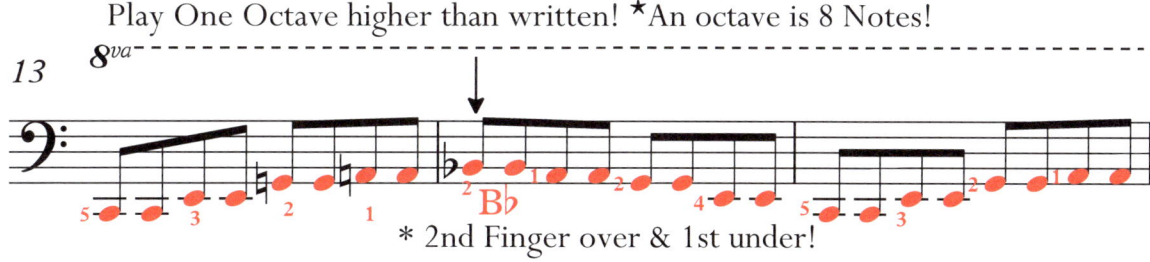

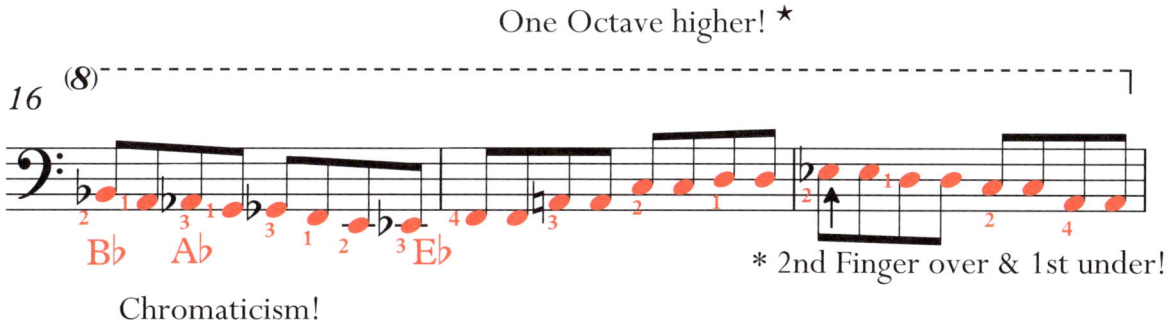

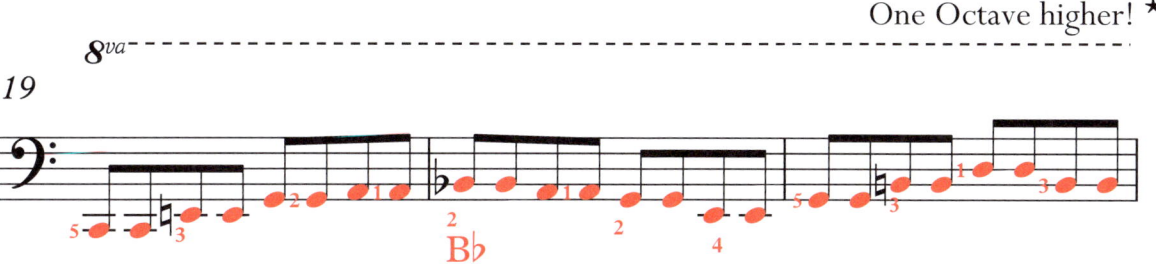

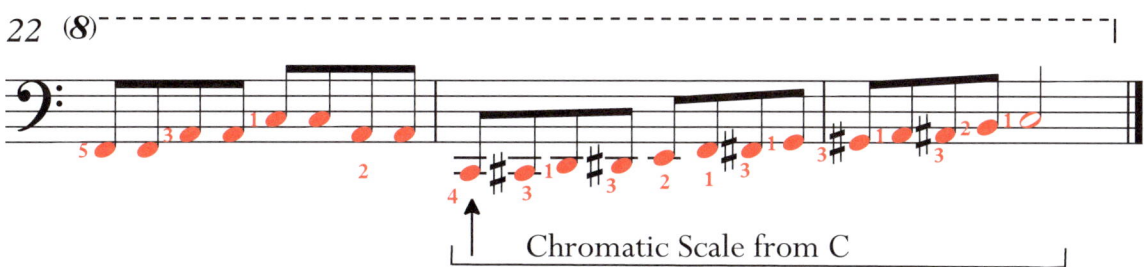

The Lockdown Blues!

An accent above or below the note head means stress that note!

A dot above or below the note head is called staccato........
Imagine a 'hot piano key' therefore lift up quickly - short & detached!

Joanne Fairclough

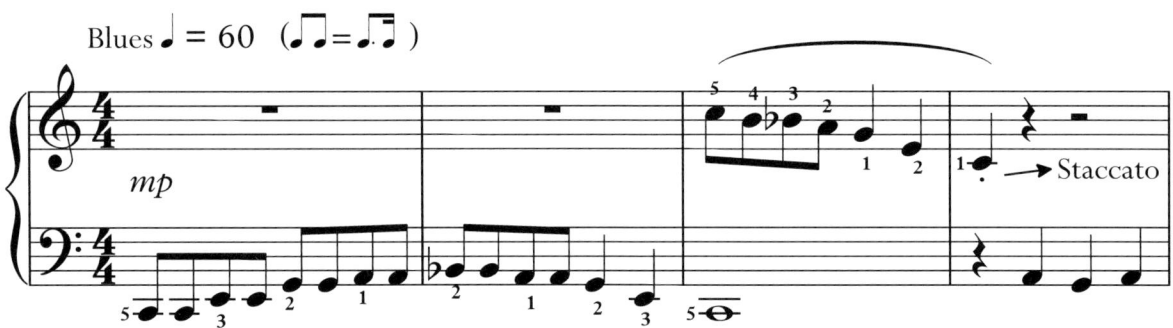

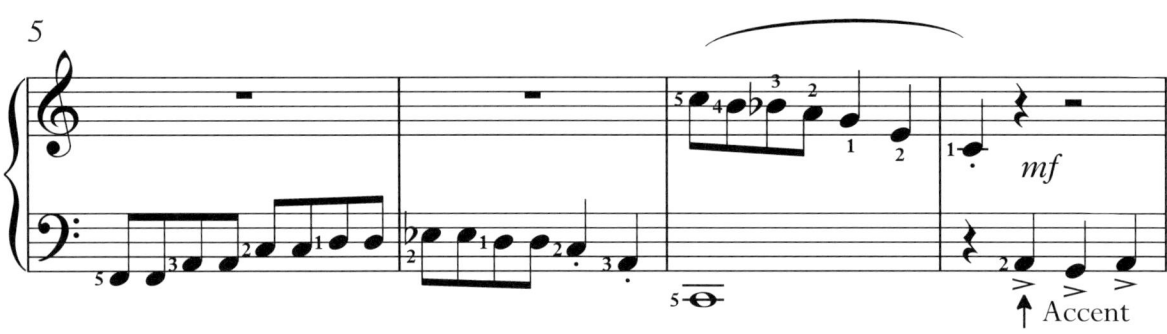

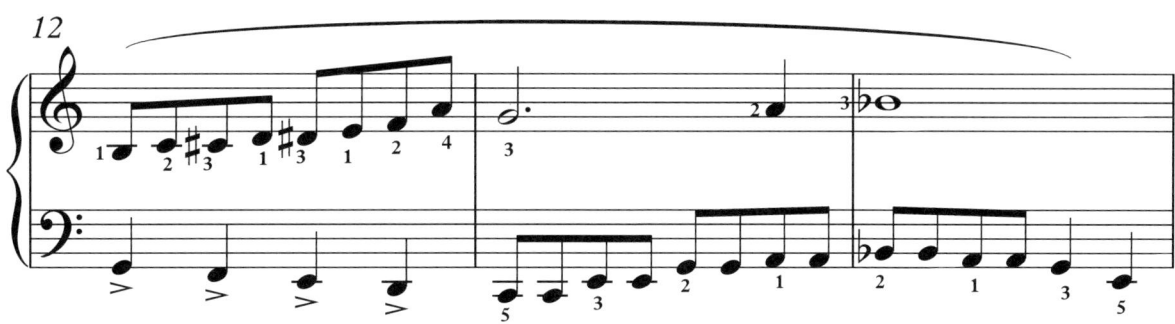

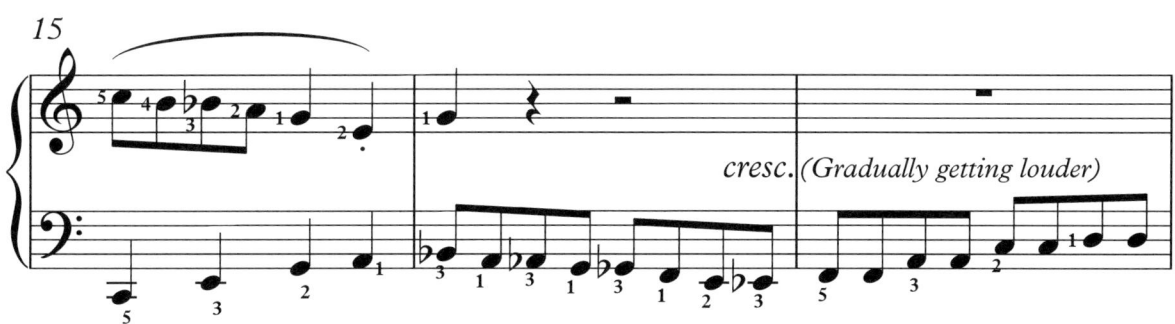

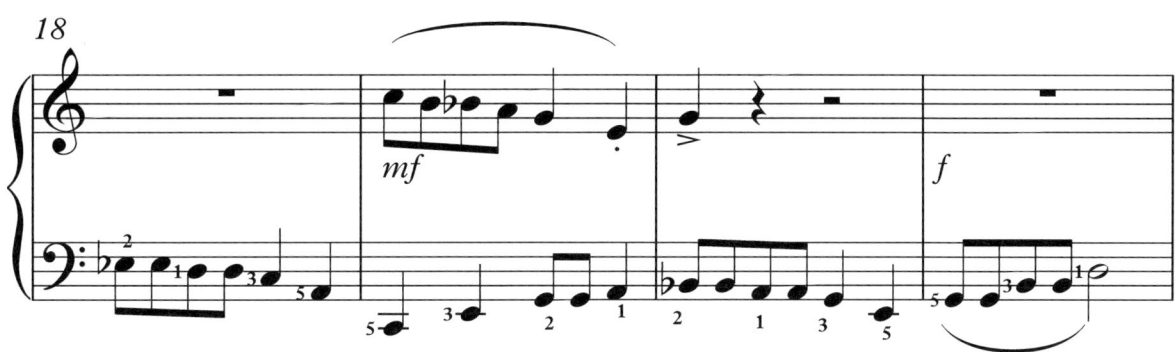

Add the sustaining pedal!

Developing Scales!
Major & Minor 2 Octaves!

The following Scales are all two Octaves!
1. Practise them separately 2 8ves
2. Practise them hands together one 8ve
3. Practise them together 2 8ves

Notice that there are no Key signatures!
The accidentals are added throughout!

♯ ♭ ♮

C Major

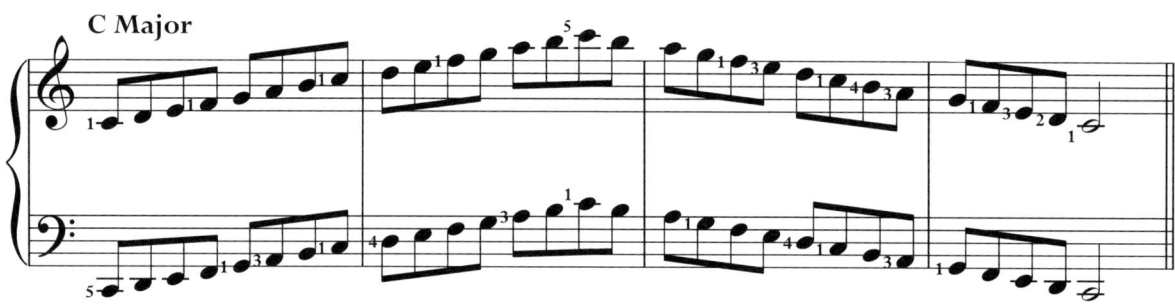

A Harmonic Minor

G Major

E F♯G F♯

E Harmonic Minor

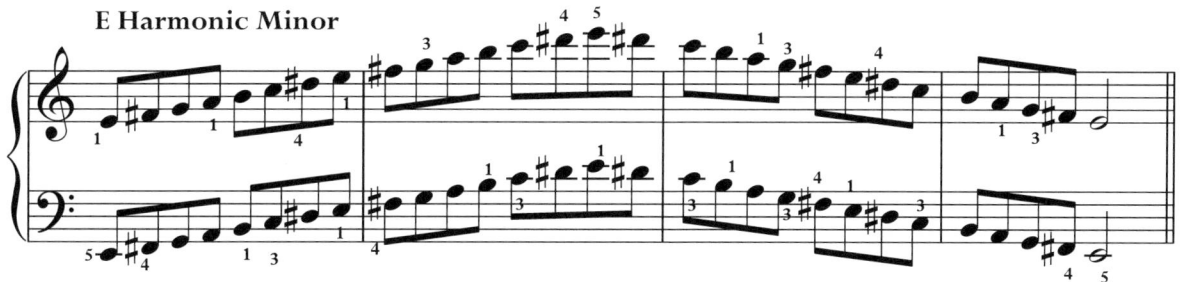

F Major

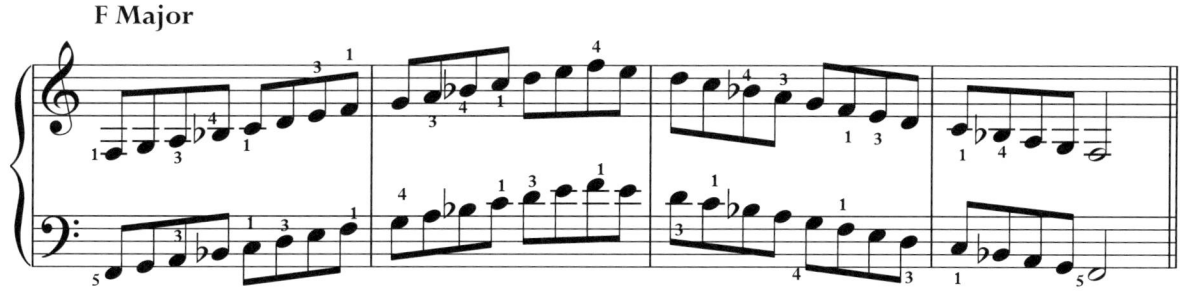

D Harmonic Minor

D Major

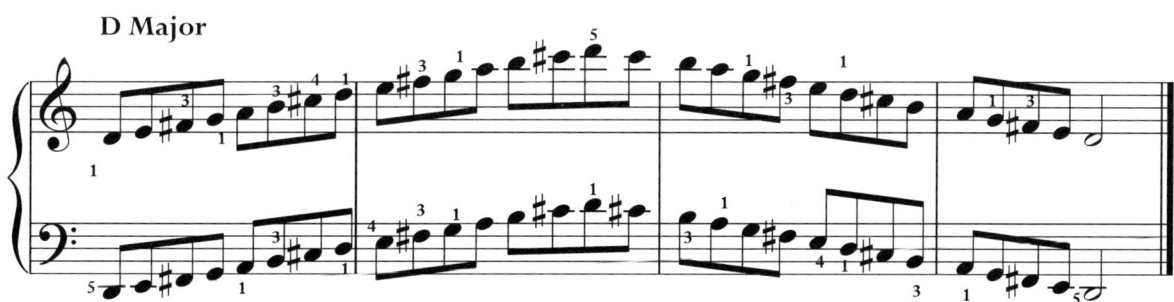